Boston
WOMEN'S
HERITAGE TRAIL

*Seven Self-guided Walks Through Four
Centuries of Boston Women's History*

*"We should have every path laid
open to woman as freely as to man."*
—Margaret Fuller

Boston Women's Heritage Trail: Seven Self-guided Walks Through Four Centuries of Boston Women's History

2006 © Boston Women's Heritage Trail
Third Edition
All rights reserved
ISBN-13: 978-1-933212-40-1
ISBN-10: 1-933212-40-3

Written by:
Polly Welts Kaufman, Jean Gibran,
Sylvia McDowell, Mary Howland Smoyer

Special assistance:
Sara Masucci, Bonnie Hurd Smith

Book design: Bonnie Hurd Smith
www.hurdsmith.com

Logo design: Ginny O'Neil (see page 55)

Contemporary photography:
Susan Wilson
www.susanwilsonphoto.com

First edition 1991 by Polly Welts Kaufman,
Patricia Morris, and Joyce Stevens, under a grant
to the Boston Public Schools from the Women's
Educational Equity Act. Second edition 1999.

Cover
Left row, top: Isabella Stewart Gardner (see page 59);
    bottom: Myrna Vasquez (see page 89)
Middle row, top: Louisa May Alcott (see page 36);
    bottom: Rose Kennedy with Joe Jr. (see page 25)
Right row, top: Edmonia Lewis (see page 14);
    bottom: Amelia Earhart (see page 48)

Back cover
Left: Chew Shee Chin (see page 45);
Middle: Lucy Stone (see page 13);
Right: Mary Eliza Mahoney (see page 38)

Inside front cover
Boston Women's Memorial (see page 73)

Inside back cover
Step on Board, featuring Harriet Tubman (see pages 76, 77)

Opposite page:
St. Paul's Church, Tremont Street

Boston WOMEN'S HERITAGE TRAIL

*Seven Self-guided Walks Through Four
Centuries of Boston Women's History*

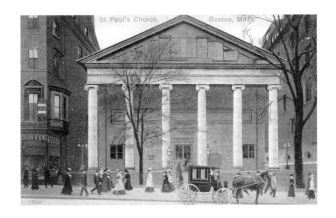

Boston Women's Heritage Trail
Boston, Massachusetts

Downtown Walk · 9

features women across the centuries, with a focus on the eighteenth century through the mid-nineteenth century. It includes women who wrote poetry, essays, and plays and spoke out publicly before members of the Massachusetts State Legislature and in Boston's halls and churches for the abolition of slavery, woman suffrage, and African American and Native American rights. Boston's downtown area is home to its business and financial institutions, as well as to a major shopping area and the Quincy Market at Faneuil Hall.

North End Walk · 25

presents the lives of women from a variety of ethnic groups. Beginning with Yankee women active in support of the Revolutionary War, the walk continues with the activities of Irish, Jewish, and Italian women in the nineteenth and twentieth centuries. The area is one of Boston's oldest neighborhoods. Its narrow streets are filled with the hustle and bustle of residents, shoppers, and tourists enjoying the Italian restaurants and groceries as well as historic sites and specialty shops.

Beacon Hill Walk · 33

starts with intense activity in the period before and after the Civil War and continues into the nineteenth century. Women writers and artists living here used their talents to support social movements ranging from anti-slavery to suffrage. The walk pays particular attention to the story of Beacon Hill's African American women and of Boston's first women doctors and professional nurses. Beacon Hill is a designated Historic District with narrow, steep, sometimes cobblestone streets, and brick homes featuring beautiful doorways and window boxes. It was first developed by the Mount Vernon Proprietors in 1795. Charles Street along its western edge includes antique and specialty shops, restaurants, and grocery stores.

South Cove/Chinatown Walk · 43

focuses on immigrant groups, most recently Chinese. The walk also includes a women's settlement house serving an earlier immigrant population, and the international programs of a Catholic sisterhood. The South Cove area, originally the South Cove of Boston Harbor, was filled in between 1833-39. Although the Chinese community began arriving in the mid-nineteenth century, large numbers of women were not allowed until the liberalization of immigration laws in the mid-twentieth century. The people of the Chinese community give the area its special spirit, along with its architecture, murals, restaurants, groceries, and shops.

Back Bay Walk, East and West, · 53, 63

originally a mudflat, was filled in with gravel brought from suburban Needham by train between 1852 and 1890. This elegant neighborhood includes Commonwealth Avenue with its tree-lined mall of grass, center walking path, and sculptures, as well as the "uptown" shopping area with high-end stores, art galleries, and restaurants. The Back Bay East Walk highlights the work of women in the arts and in education, and women who led the way in environmental protection, suffrage, and peace. The Back Bay West Walk focuses on women of the mid-nineteenth and early twentieth centuries, demonstrating the high energy devoted by women to the arts and education, pointing out educational institutions, clubs, and art associations as well as women's sculptures.

South End Walk · 75

presents a wide diversity of women, from mid-nineteenth through the twentieth centuries, particularly a flourishing African American community and their organizations. It takes us to two impressive sculptures, crafted by women, honors the area's immigrant populations including the newest group, the Latino community, and presents the work of women in settlement houses, hospitals, and schools. A Victorian neighborhood, the South End was laid out in 1801 by architect Charles Bulfinch and built on filled land. It is a designated Landmark District featuring brick and brownstone row houses, cast iron fences and railings, and streets with center parks. The South End is home to an active arts community, as well as restaurants, cafés, and shops.

Credits	91	**Acknowledgments**	98
Boston-Area Research Resources	93	**Sister Trails**	99
More About Boston Women	94	**Index**	100

Introduction

"Remember the Ladies," wrote Abigail Adams to husband, John, in 1776, "and be more generous and favorable to them than your ancestors!"

In the two centuries since Abigail's oft-quoted note, however, neither John nor the generations of men that followed did much to remember, credit, or commemorate the numerous women who helped mold and maintain the New Republic. Even in Boston, the acknowledged "Cradle of Liberty," the accomplishments of women were generally footnotes and afterthoughts, rather than the stuff of biographies, annual celebrations, and public statues.

In 1989, that all began to change when a group of Boston Public School teachers, librarians, and their students brainstormed and inaugurated the *Boston Women's Heritage Trail*. Like The Hub's two extant walks—the *Freedom Trail* and the *Black Heritage Trail*—this new historic trek promised to take visitors through fascinating slices and stories from Boston's illustrious past. Unlike its predecessors, the *Boston Women's Heritage Trail* highlighted the work of women, from household names like Abigail Adams, Phillis Wheatley, Amelia Earhart, Louisa May Alcott, and Rose Kennedy, to less-familiar leaders like Chew Shee Chin, Julia O'Connor, Clementine Langone, and Melnea Cass.

Between 1989 and 2006, both scholarly research and schoolroom projects throughout the city added more women's names and historic sites to the original four-part trail. New routes were developed and a variety of images were collected, enhancing the stories of women's lives with engaging visuals. Meanwhile, women's faces and names began to join their male colleagues in increasing numbers in memorials and statuary all around the city—a trend influenced, in part, by the work of the trail and its promoters. The result is this updated, expanded, and illustrated guide to almost four centuries of women's accomplishments in The Hub.

So what's left to do?

The answer is simple: read, walk, share, enjoy. And with a little luck, we will all "remember the ladies" a bit better each time we follow in their footsteps and wander these historic paths.

Susan Wilson
for the Boston Women's Heritage Trail Board of Directors
March 2006

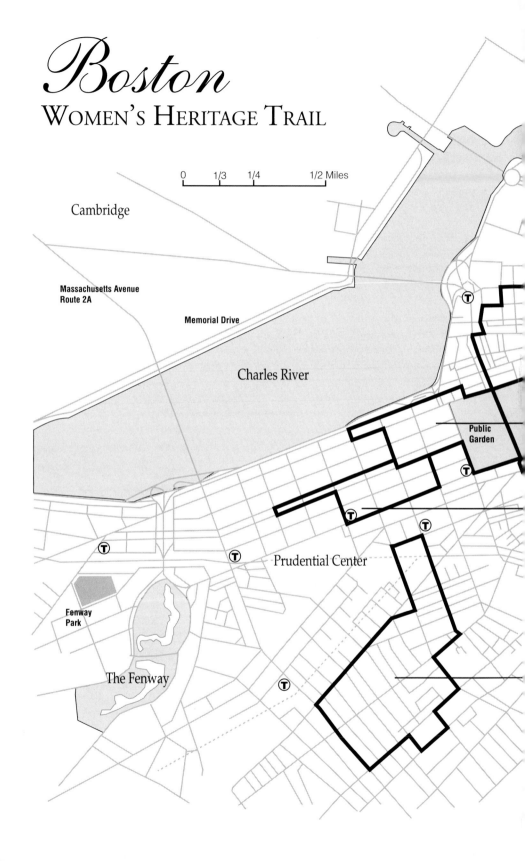

Boston
WOMEN'S HERITAGE TRAIL

0   1/3   1/4   1/2 Miles

Cambridge

Massachusetts Avenue
Route 2A

Memorial Drive

Charles River

Public
Garden

Prudential Center

Fenway
Park

The Fenway

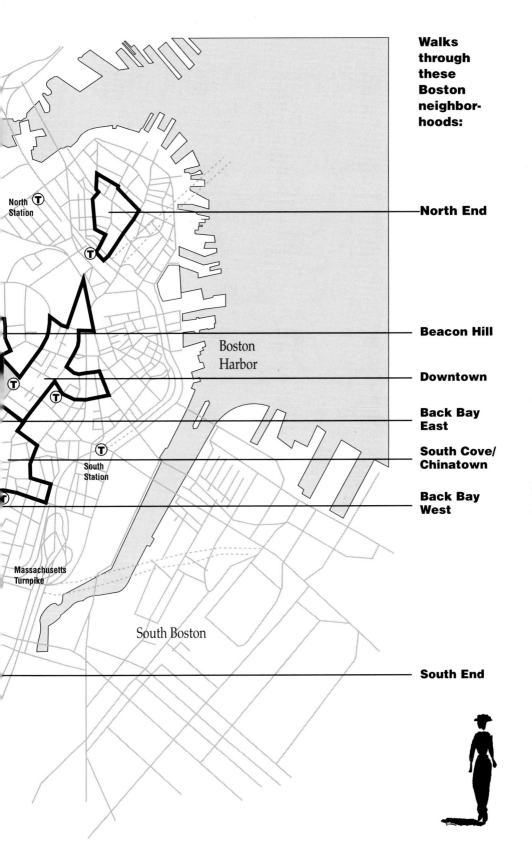

Walks through these Boston neighborhoods:

North Station

North End

Boston Harbor

Beacon Hill

Downtown

Back Bay East

South Cove/ Chinatown

South Station

Back Bay West

Massachusetts Turnpike

South Boston

South End

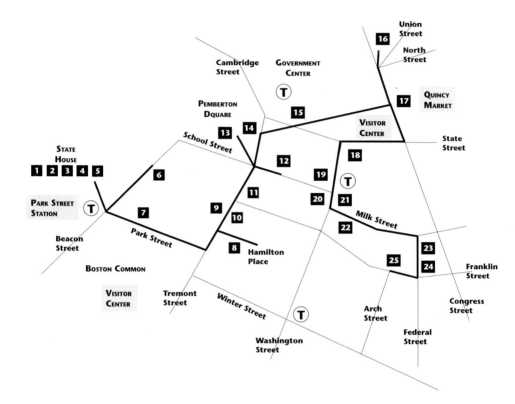

Downtown Walk

Use this map for all "D" sites

 = MBTA stop

 = historic marker

Downtown Walk

"The Search for Equal Rights"

The Downtown Walk begins at the State House, and goes past many of Boston's earliest historic sites, ending at Franklin and Washington streets, a block below Tremont Street and the Boston Common. The walk features women across the centuries, with a focus on the eighteenth century through the mid-nineteenth century. It includes women who wrote poetry, essays, and plays and spoke out publicly before members of the Massachusetts State Legislature and in Boston's halls and churches for the abolition of slavery, woman suffrage, and African American and Native American rights. Boston's downtown area is home to its business and financial institutions, as well as to a major shopping area and the Quincy Market at Faneuil Hall.

Time: 2 hours
Begins: Massachusetts State House
☞ **Directions:** Facing the State House, go left to the outside of the West Wing.

D1: Anne Hutchinson Statue
State House, Front of West Wing
Anne Hutchinson (1591-1643) was banished from Boston in the first decade of settlement because her religious views were different from those of the ruling ministers. Believing that both men and women could receive grace only from God, she accused the ministers of preaching that "good works" signified holiness. Hutchinson attracted women to prayer meetings she held in her home in part because her beliefs put women's souls on an equal footing with men's souls. She was a respected midwife and wife of an established merchant, but was banished in 1638 for heresy (see also D19). This statue, erected in 1922 as a gift of the Anne Hutchinson Memorial Association and the State Federation of Women's Clubs, was sculpted by Cyrus E. Dallin.

> "Now if you do condemn me for speaking what in my conscience I know to be the truth I must commit myself unto the Lord...."
> —Anne Hutchinson

Anne Hutchinson

D2: Mary Dyer Statue
State House, Front of East Wing
Mary Dyer (d. 1660) was a Quaker whose doctrine of Inner Light was similar to

Hutchinson's salvation by grace received directly from God. At the time, practice of the Quaker religion was not allowed in Massachusetts. She witnessed for religious freedom in Boston three times. Twice she was banished, but the third time she was hanged on Boston Common. Dyer was a friend of **Anne Hutchinson** and walked out of church beside her following Hutchinson's excommunication. This statue, erected in 1959 from a descendant's bequest, was sculpted by **Sylvia Shaw Judson** (see photo on page 102).

D3: "Hear Us" — State House Women's Leadership Project

State House, second floor south, outside Doric Hall

In 1996, the Massachusetts legislature recognized that the State House art collection included only a handful of images of women. They recommended that a new work of art be created to honor the contributions of women to public life in Massachusetts. Now permanently installed on a large wall just outside Doric Hall, the work depicts six women selected by an advisory committee. **Dorothea Dix** (1802-87) (see D5); **Lucy Stone** (1818-93) (see D7, BBW23); **Sarah Parker**

Hear Us, at the Massachusetts State House

Remond (1814-94) (see D14); **Josephine St. Pierre Ruffin** (1842-1924) (see B17); **Mary Kenney O'Sullivan** (1864-1943) (see C12); and **Florence Luscomb** (1887-1985) (see BBE17) were chosen to represent all the women who dedicated themselves to improving life in the Commonwealth. The two-toned marble panels designed by artists **Sheila Levrant de Bretteville** and **Susan Sellers** include words written by the women etched on the stone and bronze busts cast from period photographs. Historical sources were used to reveal the personal and political challenges these women faced in their struggles to bring about social change.

D4: Nurses Hall

State House, Second Floor

The statue of a Civil War nurse administering aid to a wounded soldier was a gift of the Massachusetts Daughters of Veterans in 1914. They called the nurses "Angels of Mercy and Life Amid Scenes of Conflict and Death." **Louisa May Alcott** (1832-88), author of *Little Women*, served as a Civil War nurse in Georgetown, D.C., until she contracted typhoid fever. She wrote about her experiences in *Hospital Sketches* (see B6, SE19). On the facing balcony wall is a painting honoring mothers of war by Boston artist Edward Brodney. His mother, **Sarah Brodney**, was the model for the central figure.

Two plaques behind the nurse's statue honor two individual wartime nurses: **Clara Barton** (1821-1912) and Second Lt. **Frances Slanger** (1913-44). Born in North Oxford, Massachusetts, Clara Barton is best known as the founder of the American Red Cross in 1881. During the Civil War, she administered so much direct aid and provided so many supplies that she became known as the "Angel of the Battlefield." She established the first office to coordinate information on missing soldiers. Under her leadership from 1881-1904, the Red Cross provided relief in twenty-one disasters in addition to the Spanish-American War.

Frances Slanger was the first American nurse in the European Theater to be killed in combat during World War II. A U.S. Army nurse with the 45th field hospital, she landed in Normandy with the first hospital platoon on June 9, 1944. She is also remembered for the eloquence of a letter she wrote to the *Stars and Stripes* the day before she died praising the rank and file American GI. At age seven, Slanger emigrated with her family to the U.S. from Lodz, Poland. They settled in the South End where she worked with her father peddling fruits and vegetables while attending school. She graduated from Boston's High School of Practical Arts and the Boston City Hospital School of Nursing.

D5: Angelina and Sarah Grimké; Dorothea Dix — House Chamber and Committee Rooms

State House, Third Floor
Women were considered citizens with the right to petition long before they gained the right to vote in 1920. Abolitionist **Angelina Grimké** (1805-79), who was raised by a slave-holding family in the South, spoke out against slavery on a

tour of New England with her sister **Sarah** in 1837. In 1838, she presented a women's anti-slavery petition with 20,000 signatures to a committee of the state legislature and became the first woman to publicly address the legislature. In 1843, after an eighteen-month survey of jails and poorhouses in Massachusetts, **Dorothea Dix** (1802-87) prepared a Memorial for the state legislature. "I come to place before the legislature of Massachusetts the condition of the miserable, the desolate, the outcast," Dix began, as she charged extreme cruelty in the treatment of the mentally ill. The state appropriated funds to improve one facility and she continued her investigations in many other states. During the Civil War, Dix was the superintendent of army nurses for the Union.

Directions: At the bottom of the State House steps, face Park Street and turn left on Beacon Street.

D6: The Boston Athenæum

10 1/2 Beacon Street
Many women played a role in the history of The Boston Athenæum, a library supported by memberships and thought to be the oldest library in America. Poet and celebrity **Amy Lowell** (1874-1925) was the first woman to be appointed to the Board of Directors. As a girl, Lowell had free run of the Athenæum. In 1903 when the trustees threatened to tear down the building, Amy Lowell led the protest. Her poetry flourished when, during a sojourn in Paris, she discovered French symbolism as expressed in the branch of poetry called "Imagism." She edited works of poetry, as well as bringing out collections of her own work.

The Athenæum's art collection includes: *Puck and Owl*, a sculpture by **Harriet Hosmer** (1830-1908) (see N11);

Dorothea Dix

a portrait of **Hannah Adams** (1755-1831), a scholar and author who was the first woman to be given reading privileges at the library; and a portrait by John Singer Sargent of **Annie Adams Fields** (1834-1915). Fields was a noted writer, poet, and social philanthropist, who conducted a literary salon (see B18).

☞ *Directions: Return to Park Street noting the monument to the 54th African American Civil War regiment and its leader, Robert Gould Shaw, by sculptor Augustus St. Gaudens.*

The Boston Athenæum's Fifth Floor Reading Room

D7: *Woman's Journal* and 9 to 5 Office Workers' Union
5 Park Street

The offices of the *Woman's Journal*, the newspaper published by the American Woman Suffrage Association, and the New England Women's Club, one of the first clubs for women in the country, were in another building on this site. Edited by **Lucy Stone** (1818-93), the *Journal* chose office space as close to the seat of power—the State House—as possible. Stone petitioned annually for woman suffrage. In 1879 she testified: "In this very State House, how often have women looked down from the gallery while our lawmakers voted down our rights, and heard them say, 'Half an hour is time enough to waste on it,'...[and then] turn eagerly to consider such a question as what shall be the size of a barrel of cranberries...[taking] plenty of time to consider that." Stone had been one of the first Massachusetts women to receive a college degree when she graduated from Oberlin College in 1847. When she married Henry Blackwell she became the first married woman to officially keep her maiden name, leading to the late nineteenth-century coining of the term "a Lucy Stoner" to mean a woman who stood up for her rights. Lucy Stone is one of three women chosen to be portrayed in the Boston Women's Memorial (see BBW23) and one of six to be memorialized in the State House (see D3).

Alice Stone Blackwell (1857-1950), Stone's daughter, edited the *Journal* in a building on Copley Square (see BBW5) for twenty-five

Office of the *Woman's Journal* on Park Street

years until suffrage was granted in 1920.

In 1973, a trade union for women office workers named *9 to 5* held its first monthly meetings in this building now owned by the Paulist Fathers. A member decided to organize after her boss walked into the office and said, "Well, I guess there's no one here." *9 to 5* now meets at 145 Tremont Street and shares space with Local 925 of the Services Employees Union.

dressmakers, like **Josephine McCluskey**, took on new names— she became "Miss Delavenue." The area also supported Dress Reform Parlors in the 1880s, where women could be freed from the restrictive fashions of the day. They could purchase or buy patterns for such items as the "emancipation waist."

☞ *Directions: Return to Tremont Street and cross it again.*

"*We, the people of the United States. Which 'We the people'? The women were not included.*"
—Lucy Stone

Lucy Stone

D9: Abiah Franklin and "Mother Goose" — Granary Burying Ground

Abiah Franklin (1667-1752), mother of Benjamin Franklin, was honored by her famous son when he erected the central high granite obelisk in memory of his parents. She raised 13 children, including Benjamin and **Jane Franklin Mecom** (see D22) and was called "a discreet and virtuous woman." Tradition states that **Elizabeth Foster Vergoose**,

☞ *Directions: Continue down Park Street. Cross Tremont Street to Hamilton Place.*

D8: Dress Reform Parlors and Milliners

Hamilton Place
The short streets running between Tremont and Washington Streets— including Hamilton Place, Winter Street, and Temple Place—contained shops for women in the late nineteenth and early twentieth centuries. Many women were successful proprietors of dressmaking and millinery shops, including Irish-born **Ellen Hartnett**, who rose from being a millinery worker in 1860 to a shop owner with capital twenty-five years later. In order to secure the best class of customers, some

"*If we ask ourselves Why is the subject of dress of such consequence? I think the answer will follow, Because a comparatively unimportant and external thing has come to stand as of the very first importance to the great majority of women...It was...painful to hear a devout woman, of years and wide experience say, 'I believe that the majority of women, if entering heaven to-day, would ask, not 'Where is my Lord?' but 'What do they wear there?'*"
—Abby May

known as "Mother Goose," is buried here. Widowed, she lived with her eldest daughter and entertained her grandchildren with nursery rhymes. Her son-in-law, printer Thomas Fleet, reportedly published them as *Songs for the Nursery* or *Mother Goose's Melodies*.

☞ *Directions: Look across the street.*

Edmonia Lewis

D10: Edmonia Lewis Studio

Corner of Bromfield and Tremont Streets (now Suffolk University Law School)
The studio of **Edmonia Lewis** (1845-ca. 1909), a member of the colony of women sculptors in Rome gathering around **Charlotte Cushman** (1816-76) in the mid-nineteenth century (see N11), was located in a former building at this site from 1863-65. As a child, Lewis, who had both African American and Chippewa ancestry, lived with her Chippewa mother's people. Although she was born free, her favorite subject for her sculpture was freedom from slavery, demonstrated in *Forever Free*, a sculpture depicting a man and woman breaking their chains, made as a tribute to abolitionist William Lloyd Garrison. It is now on display at the Howard University Gallery of Art. Her most popular work was a bust of Colonel Robert Gould

Shaw, the white commander of the African American 54th Massachusetts Infantry during the Civil War. Lewis's identification with her Chippewa heritage caused her also to revere and create a bust of Henry Wadsworth Longfellow, author of the poem, *Hiawatha*. The sculpture is now owned by the Fogg Art Museum at Harvard University.

☞ *Directions: Continue along Tremont Street.*

D11: Tremont Temple Women Lecturers

88 Tremont Street
In an earlier building on this site, nineteenth century women held many meetings urging the abolition of slavery, adoption of woman suffrage, and temperance reform. **Mary Rice Livermore** (1820-1905) was a prominent national lecturer after the Civil War who often spoke at Tremont Temple. Her first speech there was in 1869 when her subject was woman suffrage. Her Boston speeches in 1874 led to the founding of the Massachusetts Women's Christian Temperance Union for which she served as president for ten years. Livermore was the first editor of the *Woman's Journal*. She later held the office of president of the American Woman Suffrage Association and was first president of the Association for the Advancement of Women.

"This is woman's hour, with all its sweet amenities and its moral and religious reforms."
—Mary Baker Eddy

Mary Baker Eddy

Here, in March 1885, **Mary Baker Eddy** (1821-1910), founder of the Church of Christ, Scientist, was given ten minutes to respond to a barrage of criticism from members of the Boston clergy. Her ideas about God as father-mother and of man and woman as co-equals—both created in God's image—angered the ministers of the time. Her book, *Science and Health*, was a best seller. In the years following her talk, Eddy emerged as one of the most important women reformers of her day, pioneering in the field of mind-body medicine. Soon after she spoke in Tremont Temple, she wrote, "Let it not be heard in Boston that woman...has no rights which man is bound to respect....This is woman's hour, with all its sweet amenities and its moral and religious reforms" (see also SE14).

☞ *Directions: Continue along Tremont Street. Turn right on School Street.*

Julia
Harrington
Duff

D12: Boston School Committeewomen

Old City Hall, 45 School Street

Women were elected to the Boston School Committee before they could vote. In 1875, after a drive by the New England Women's Club, six women took their seats on the Boston School Committee elected by Boston men. Although the Committee was reduced from 116 to 24 members the following year, four women were reelected including **Lucretia Crocker**

Abby
W. May

(1829-86) (see SE8), who later became the first woman supervisor in the Boston Public Schools, and **Abby May** (1829-88). May succeeded in starting a separate Latin School for girls, but it was not until 1972 that the two Latin schools became co-educational. When May was defeated for reelection, women all over Massachusetts petitioned the legislature and won the right to vote for school board members, starting in 1879 (see also D25).

Julia Harrington Duff (1859-1932) of Charlestown, a former Boston School teacher, was the first Irish-American woman to be elected to the Boston School Committee in 1900. Her rallying cry, "Boston schools for Boston girls," expressed her belief that Yankee teachers from outside the city were being hired in preference to the young Catholic women graduates of Boston's Normal School. Boston women teachers pressed for their rights. Among the women challenging the 1880s School Committee regulation that women resign upon marriage were **Grace Lonergan Lorch** (1903-74) and **Suzanne Revaleon Green**. Green's husband, a lawyer, succeeded in having his wife and two other married teachers reinstated to their teaching positions. The regulation remained on the books, however, until 1953 when a state law required its removal.

☞ *Directions: Return to and cross Tremont Street. Turn right. Go up the stairs through Center Plaza to Pemberton Square. On your left is D13.*

Jennie Loitman Barron

D13: Women Judges

Municipal Court House, Pemberton Square
Jennie Loitman Barron (1891-1969)
became the state's first full-time woman
judge in 1934. She served for thirty
years, twenty in the Boston Municipal
Court and ten in the Superior Court.
As a lawyer representing the League of
Women Voters, she successfully argued
for women's service on juries. Before she
became a judge, Barron served on the
Boston School Committee in the late
1920s, where she focused attention on
substandard school conditions.

☞ *Directions: Look to the right of the
Court House for the former location
of the Howard Athenæum.*

D14: Sarah Parker Remond and the Howard Athenæum

Pemberton Square
Sarah Parker Remond, the grand-
daughter of a free black who fought in
the Revolutionary War, committed her
first act of public resistance at the Howard
Athenæum. In 1853, Remond, who lived
in Salem, had purchased tickets by mail
for a performance at the Howard. When
she arrived, the theater would not seat her
in the seats she had paid for but, instead,

made her sit in the segregated gallery.
She refused, departed, and later sued
the theater, winning $500 in damages.
Remond went on to become an
international anti-slavery lecturer
(see also D3).

The Howard Athenæum was opened
in 1846 with the first cushioned theater
seats in Boston. It was a fashionable
theater, playing opera and drama until
1870 when it turned to vaudeville. The
building was demolished in 1962.

Sarah Parker
Remond

☞ *Directions: Walk down the steps
through Center Plaza to Cambridge
Street. Cross to City Hall Plaza.*

D15: Abigail Adams, Mercy Otis Warren, and Brattle Square

City Hall Plaza, Cambridge Street
The Boston City Hall Plaza covers the
same ground as the eighteenth century
Brattle Square. From 1768 to 1771,
Abigail Adams (1744-1817) lived in
two locations in and near Brattle Square
with her husband, attorney John Adams,
and their family. It was a period of
increasing family responsibilities for her.
Her five children were born between
1765 and 1772. The family lived there
during the Boston Massacre, which
took place nearby—just outside the

Abigail Adams

Old State House—in 1770. After John Adams successfully defended the British soldiers involved in the incident, his health declined. The family moved back to their farm in Braintree (now Quincy) the following year, but returned to Boston in 1772. They were in Boston during the Boston Tea Party in 1773, but by 1774 the Adamses had moved back to the farm permanently because John began traveling for the new Republic—first as a delegate to the Continental Congress in Philadelphia.

> "If peace and unanimity are cherished, and the equalization of liberty, and the equity and energy of law, maintained by harmony and justice, the present representative government may stand for ages a luminous monument of republican wisdom, virtue and integrity. The principles of the revolution ought ever to be the pole-star of the statesman...not only for the benefit of existing society, but with an eye to that fidelity which is due posterity."
> —Mercy Otis Warren

Abigail Adams became well known as a critical thinker and correspondent with her husband, who was away from the farm for much of the next ten years. She managed the farm, their large family, and their financial affairs. Abigail Adams is one of three women chosen to be portrayed in the Boston Women's Memorial (see BBW23).

Among Abigail Adams's correspondents was **Mercy Otis Warren** (1728-1814), probably the first published women historian in the U.S. In 1805, she published a three-volume history of the American Revolution. She also published several satirical plays.

Mercy Otis Warren

☞ *Directions: Walk across City Hall Plaza Go down the steps, cross Congress Street to Faneuil Hall. Turn left. Cross North Street into Carmen Park, between Congress and Union Streets.*

D16: Holocaust Memorial
Carmen Park

Dozens of prominent Boston women were involved in planning and funding the New England Holocaust Memorial, some of them survivors of Nazi concentration camps who have found new lives in Boston. The Memorial was dedicated in October 1995 to foster the memory of, and reflection on, one of the great tragedies of modern times. The Memorial features six luminous glass towers etched with six million numbers to remind visitors of those who perished during the Holocaust, or Shoah, from 1933-45. In total, the Memorial honors all eleven million people who perished because of their race, religion, nationality, physical disability or sexual preference, as well as those who courageously aided death camp survivors. The Memorial's dedication includes the words, "...know that wherever prejudice, discrimination and victimization are tolerated, evil like the Holocaust can happen again."

☞ *Directions: Return to Faneuil Hall. Note the statue of patriot Sam Adams by sculptor* **Anne Whitney** *(see B15).*

D17: Protest Meetings and Faneuil Hall

Quincy Market

Faneuil Hall and the adjoining Quincy Market are the historic locations of Boston's great women's fairs and protest meetings. The Anti-Slavery Bazaars, sponsored by the Female Anti-Slavery Societies, were held there in the 1830s and 1840s. In September 1840, women held a seven-day fair to raise money to complete the building of the Bunker Hill monument. Inspired by **Sarah Josepha Hale** (1820-79), the women raised $30,000 (see N7). Among the women's suffrage meetings held in Faneuil Hall was a New England Woman's Tea Party, sponsored on the centennial of the Boston Tea Party by the New England Woman Suffrage Association. They invited the public to join them in the celebration, noting that women were still subject to "taxation without representation." In an alcove behind the stage, note the bust of **Lucy Stone**, a main speaker at the Tea Party (see D7, BBW23).

Suzette "Bright Eyes" LaFleshe (1854-1903), an Omaha Indian, inspired the Indian Rights Movement when she spoke in Faneuil Hall in December 1879. LaFlesche, wearing native dress and a bear-claw necklace, protested the reservation system: "Did our Creator...intend that men created in his own image should be ruled over by another set of his creatures?" After hearing Bright Eyes speak in Boston, many Boston women became her supporters. **Helen Hunt Jackson** (1830-85) was inspired by her speech to write *A Century of Dishonor*, a book that cited injustices to the Indian peoples, and works of fiction about Native Americans including *Ramona*.

Working women saw Faneuil Hall as a place for a forum for their demands. In 1903, the Women's Trade Union League was founded in Faneuil Hall (see C16). Massachusetts nurses also chose the hall to rally for professional status in 1903 when they founded the Massachusetts Nurses Association. Among the organizers was **Lucy Lincoln Drown** (1847-1934), superintendent of nurses at Boston City Hospital from 1885 to 1910. In 1919, the call for the women telephone operators' strike brought two thousand angry women to the hall (see C4).

Suzette "Bright Eyes" LaFleshe

☞ *Directions: Continue up Congress Street. Turn right on State Street noting the Old State House (which is managed by The Bostonian Society) and the National Park Service Visitor Center. Turn left on Washington Street.*

Elizabeth Murray

"I'd rather [be] a useful member of society than all of the fine delicate creatures of the age."
—Elizabeth Murray

D18: Elizabeth Murray, Corn Hill and Queen Street

(now, roughly, Court and Washington Streets)

Born in Scotland, **Elizabeth Murray** (1726-85) came to Boston in 1749. At age twenty-three she established a business selling imported cloth and dry goods from Great Britain. She proved to be such a resourceful business woman that she soon earned enough money to be entirely self-sufficient—a rare achievement for a colonial woman. Although she married three times, Murray remained childless. Still, she oversaw the education and upbringing of her nieces, kindling in them a spirit of self-reliance and self-esteem. She helped them and other needy women set up shops of their own. Murray once wrote to a friend, "I'd rather [be] a useful member of society than all of the fine delicate creatures of the age."

☞ *Directions: Continue on Washington Street. A plaque in Spring Lane, on the left, marks the site of the home of* **Mary Chilton Winslow** *(d.1679), a Mayflower passenger in 1620.*

D19: Old Corner Bookstore

Corner of School and Washington Streets

Anne Hutchinson lived in a house on this site in the mid 1630s across from Governor John Winthrop. It was here that she conducted women's prayer meetings (see D1). In the mid-nineteenth century, the present building, known as the Old Corner Bookstore, housed the publishing firm of Ticknor and Fields. **Annie Adams Fields** (1834-1915), wife of publisher James T. Fields, conducted a literary salon for authors in the Fields' home on Charles Street (see B18).

D20: Irish Famine Memorial and Annie Sullivan

Corner of School and Washington Streets

The Irish Famine Memorial was dedicated in 1998 to commemorate the 150th anniversary of the Irish potato famine. It honors the arrival of Irish immigrants to Boston and their contributions to the city. Created by sculptor Robert Shure, the sculptures depict a starving family in Ireland begging for help, and one arriving in America.

Irish Famine Memorial, detail

Annie Sullivan (left) and Helen Keller

> "*Children require guidance and sympathy far more than instruction.*" —Annie Sullivan

Among the Irish women honored by the Boston Women's Heritage Trail is **Annie Sullivan Macy** (1866-1936), known as the gifted teacher of **Helen Keller** (1880-1968). Born to poor Irish immigrants to Massachusetts, Sullivan progressively became blind. After the death of her mother and her father's abandonment, she entered an orphanage. In 1880, a supervisor placed her in the Perkins School for the Blind in South Boston. Two operations improved her eyesight enough so she could read, and Sullivan graduated as valedictorian of her class. She became the teacher of Helen Keller, who came from an advantaged family but could not hear, see, or speak. Sullivan devoted her life to Keller, who became a national celebrity, and saw Keller through her education and early career.

D21: Old South Meeting House and Phillis Wheatley

310 Washington Street

When Old South, the site of mass protest meetings in Revolutionary Boston, was slated for demolition a hundred years later, a group of women bought the building (but not the land) to protect it. Philanthropist **Mary Tileston Hemenway** (1820-94) then contributed more than half the sum needed to preserve it, becoming an early leader in historic preservation.

Phillis Wheatley (ca. 1753-84), the first African American poet to be published in book form, was a member of Old South. While still a child, she was purchased as a slave by the Wheatley family. Her poetry reflects her love of freedom: "Should you...wonder from whence my love of Freedom sprung...I, young in life, was snatched from Afric's fancy'd happy seat...such, such my case. And can I then but pray Others may never feel tyrannic sway?" Phillis Wheatley is one of three women chosen to be portrayed in the Boston Women's Memorial (see BBW23). An exhibit depicting her life is permanently displayed here. For the site marking her landing place, see C6.

Phillis Wheatley

> "*Poetry is the voice through which I speak to the world. I was taken from my parents ...at the age of seven, my only memory being one of my mother pouring out water before the sun rose. That was in 1761, when I was transported as a slave to Boston....*"
> —Phillis Wheatley

☞ *Directions: Turn left on Milk Street.*

Birthplace of Jane Franklin Mecom

D22: Birthplace of
Jane Franklin Mecom

(and Benjamin Franklin), 17 Milk Street
Jane Franklin Mecom (1712-94),
Benjamin Franklin's sister and favorite
family correspondent, survived the
trials of raising nine children and many
grandchildren in eighteenth-century
Boston. After Mecom's husband died in
1765, she opened a boarding house near
the Old State House, where legislators
stayed frequently and kept her informed
about local and national political issues.
At the age of seventy-six she wrote: "I have
a good clean House to live in...I go to bed
Early lye warm & comfortable Rise Early
to a good Fire have my Brakfast directly
and Eate it with a good Apetite and then
read or Work...we live frugaly Bake all our
own Bread...a Friend sitts and chats a litle
in the Evening...."

☞ *Directions: Continue down
Milk Street to Federal Street.
Turn right.*

D23: Susanna Rowson and
Federal Street Theatre

Federal Street
Susanna Haswell Rowson (1760-1824),
a playwright and an actress at the Federal
Street Theatre, was
the author of the
first American
best-selling novel,
*Charlotte Temple,
A Tale of Truth.*
Rowson arrived
in America when
she was six, but
her father was a Loyalist
and during the Revolution
they returned to England. Not long after
her marriage to William Rowson, Susanna
returned to America and settled in Boston
where they both acted at the Federal Street
Theatre. For the five years following 1796,
she performed 129 different parts in 126
productions, many of which she wrote
herself. Her next venture was to set up a
Young Ladies Academy in 1797 near the
Theatre. Rowson moved the school out of
Boston but later returned. Her academy
was one of the first to offer girls education
above the elementary level and included
instruction in music and public speaking.

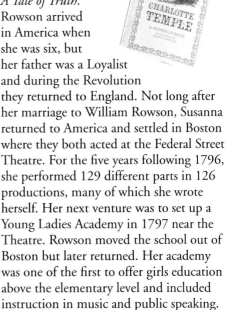

Another woman playwright whose
plays were performed at the Federal Street
Theatre in 1795 and 1796 was **Judith
Sargent Murray** (see D25). Her satirical
plays, *The Medium or Happy Tea-Party*

Federal Street Theatre, ca. 1795

(later renamed *The Medium, or Virtue Triumphant*) and *The Traveller Returned*, addressed class structure and gender roles in the New Republic.

Public speakers lecturing at the Federal Street Theatre included **Deborah Sampson** (1760-1827), considered to be America's first female soldier. In 1802, Sampson electrified the crowd as she told her story of fighting in the Revolutionary War for eighteen months disguised as a man named Robert Shurtleff.

☞ *Directions: Continue to the corner of Federal and Franklin Streets.*

> *"A piercing voice of grief and wrong,/ Goes upward from the groaning earth!/ Oh true and holy Lord! how long?/In majesty and might come forth!"*
> —Maria Weston Chapman, from
> *Songs of the Free*

D24: Federal Street Church

100 Federal Street
Among the more well-known Boston women who attended William Ellery Channing's Federal Street Church were abolitionists **Maria Weston Chapman** (1806-85) and **Eliza Lee Cabot Follen**. Chapman, a founder of the Boston Female Anti-Slavery Society, was a supporter of abolitionist William Lloyd Garrison, publisher of the famed abolitionist newspaper *The Liberator*. An inspired organizer and fundraiser, Chapman ran twenty-two yearly anti-slavery fairs in Boston beginning in 1834. One of her colleagues in this venture was **Lydia Maria Child** (1802-80) whose 1833 publication, *An Appeal in Behalf of that Class of Americans called Africans*, was the first book to advocate an immediate end to slavery. Chapman's fairs became a model

for women in other parts of the country to raise money for the abolitionist cause. Chapman also published several important anti-slavery tracts including *How Can I Help Abolish Slavery?* and *Right and Wrong in Massachusetts*. With Garrison, Maria Chapman supported women's full participation in abolitionist work— including public speaking, which had been condemned in a pastoral letter from the Congregational ministers of Massachusetts as being outside women's God-ordained sphere. In 1840, Chapman was elected to the executive committee of the American Anti-Slavery Society.

Eliza Lee Cabot Follen (1787-1860) was best known for her anti-slavery writings including *Anti-Slavery Hymns and Songs* and *A Letter to Mothers in Free States*. In A Letter, Follen wrote, "...what can women,—what can we mothers do?... you can do everything; I repeat, you can abolish slavery. Let every mother take the subject to heart, as one in which she has a personal concern. In the silence of the night, let her listen to the slave-mothers crying to her for help...." Much of Follen's writing was designed for children, including songs, poems, and stories that carried a moral lesson.

☞ *Directions: Turn right up Franklin Street to Arch Street.*

Franklin Place, The Tontine Crescent

D25: Franklin Place and Home of Judith Sargent Murray

Franklin and Arch Streets

The Tontine Crescent was a fashionable place to live in late eighteenth and early nineteenth-century Boston. The long row of elegant townhouses, designed by Boston architect Charles Bulfinch, was built in 1793 and named Franklin Place after Benjamin Franklin. With the opening of the Back Bay for settlement, they declined in fashion and were demolished in 1872 after the Great Fire. Franklin Street still retains the curve of the buildings.

Among the notable women who lived there was **Judith Sargent Murray** (1751-1820), a native of Gloucester, who moved with her husband, John Murray, to No. 5 Franklin Place in 1794 (see N9). Judith Sargent Murray was already a successful writer, publishing a regular column ("The Gleaner") in the *Massachusetts Magazine*, a new literary monthly. Using a male persona, Judith expressed her opinions on female equality, education, federalism, and republicanism. She wrote that not only should a woman be educated to be "the sensible and informed" companion of men, but she should also be equipped to earn her own living. Murray saw the many new female academies as inaugurating "a new era in female history." In 1798, she published her "Gleaner" essays in a book she also called *The Gleaner*, selling it to a list of subscribers including John Adams and George Washington. *The Gleaner* became a minor classic, and Murray became the first woman in America to self-publish. She was also a poet, publishing in various Boston periodicals under the pen names "Honora Martesia" and "Constantia." An avid letter writer, the copies of letters Murray wrote from 1765-1818 (ages 14-67) were discovered in 1984, and offer a new eyewitness account of early American history.

Judith Sargent Murray

> "The idea of the incapability of women is…totally inadmissible….To argue against facts, is indeed contending with both wind and tide; and, borne down by accumulating examples, conviction of the utility of the present plans will pervade the public mind, and not a dissenting voice will be heard."
> —Judith Sargent Murray

Abby May (1829-88), also an advocate for women's rights, lived at 5 Franklin Place with her family as a young woman. Among her many achievements, May succeeded in starting a separate Latin School for girls (see D12) and served as one of the first women on the Boston School Committee.

☞ *Directions: Continue up Franklin Street to Washington Street. If you turn left on Washington Street to West Street, you can join the Chinatown loop of the Boston Women's Heritage Trail. If you turn left on Washington Street and right on Winter Street, you will arrive at the Boston Common near Park Street below the State House, where you started the Downtown Walk.*

End of Walk

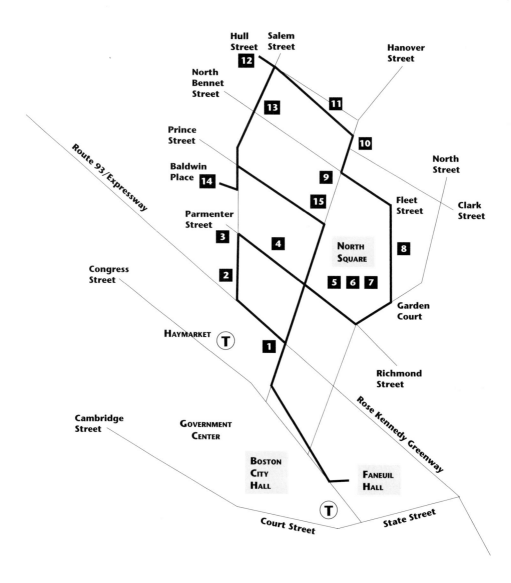

North End Walk

Use this map for all "N" sites

 = MBTA stop

 = historic marker

North End Walk

"A Diversity of Cultures"

The North End Walk starts at Faneuil Hall, crosses the new Rose Kennedy Greenway, and winds through the narrow streets of the North End, often paralleling the Freedom Trail. The walk presents the lives of women from a variety of ethnic groups. Beginning with Yankee women active in support of the Revolutionary War, the walk continues with the activities of Irish, Jewish, and Italian women in the nineteenth and twentieth centuries. The area is one of Boston's oldest neighborhoods. Its narrow streets are filled with the hustle and bustle of residents, shoppers, and tourists enjoying the Italian restaurants and groceries as well as historic sites and specialty shops.

Time: 1 1/2 hours
Begins: Faneuil Hall
☞ **Directions:** Follow the Freedom Trail's red line toward the North End to the Rose Kennedy Greenway at Hanover Street.

Rose Kennedy with Joe Jr.

N1: Rose Kennedy Greenway and North End Parks

The Rose Kennedy Greenway caps the Central Artery Transportation Project (Big Dig). This entrance connects the North End with Government Center and downtown Boston. The entire greenway, which stretches from the North Station to a few blocks below the South Station, consists of three hundred acres of landscaped open space containing fourteen parks.

The Greenway honors **Rose Fitzgerald Kennedy** (1890-1995) who was born in the North End and lived there as a child (see N8, 10). Her father, John F. Fitzgerald, was the first American-born Irish Democrat to be elected mayor of Boston, serving from 1905-07 and from 1910-1914. As the eldest child of six, Rose was often at her father's side in public. Despite her wish to attend Wellesley College, her family sent her to Catholic schools, including Manhattanville College. She married Joseph Kennedy in 1914 and nine children followed. She served as ambassador's wife to the Court of St. James from 1937 until the outbreak of World War II.

Rose Kennedy is especially remembered as the mother of President John F. Kennedy, Attorney General Robert Kennedy, and Senator Edward Kennedy. She devoted her life to raising her children and was active in supporting her sons' political campaigns as well as programs for children with special needs.

☞ *Directions: Cross the Greenway at Hanover Street and turn left to Salem Street.*

N2: Goody Glover, Goody Glover Tavern

Beginning of Salem Street

The tavern takes its name from **Goody Glover** (d. 1688), an Irish servant in the John Goodwin family who was accused by Cotton Mather of witchcraft and hanged in Boston. A practicing Roman Catholic, Glover was named as a witch when four of her five children fell ill without apparent cause. During her trial, she protested by speaking only Irish, even though she knew English. A plaque remembering her as the first Catholic martyr in Massachusetts is located on Our Lady of Victories Eucharistic Shrine on Isabella Street in the South End.

N3: Home of Sophie Tucker

Formerly 22 Salem Street

Born Sophie Abuza in Russia, **Sophie Tucker** (1884-1966) emigrated as a small child to the North End, where her family joined a growing Jewish community on lower Salem Street. After the family moved to Hartford, she began singing in her father's kosher restaurant. By the time she was seventeen, she was performing in New York City and on her way to headlines in vaudeville. Her signature song was *Some of These Days*. In later life she became a philanthropist for Jewish causes.

☞ *Directions: Continue up Salem Street to Parmenter Street. Turn right.*

> *"Playing in the dirt is the royalty of childhood."* —Kate Gannett Wells

Children in the North End Union's sandbox, ca. 1886

N4: Boston Public Library; North End Union

25 Parmenter Street

Across the street from the North End branch of the Boston Public Library is the former location of the North End Union founded in 1892 to meet the needs of Irish, Jewish, and Italian immigrant families. Boston's first public playground, a sand garden, was started by a committee of philanthropic women in the yard of the Chapel that occupied the site in 1886 (see plaque). "Playing in the dirt is the royalty of childhood," said committee member **Kate Gannett Wells** (1838-1911). Mothers supervised children at first; later, employed kindergarten teachers read to the children and taught them crafts and led them in marching and singing. The public library branch is built on the former site of the **Charlotte Cushman** School named for the renowned nineteenth century actress who was born in a house on this site in 1816 (see N11). Inside is a diorama of the Ducal Palace in Venice made by artist **Louise Stimson** (1890-1981) in 1949 (see BBW1).

☞ *Directions: Cross Hanover Street to Richmond Street. Turn left on North Street, bearing left to North Square.*

Clementine
Poto Langone

N5: Poto Family Grocery Store

33 North Square

The former home and grocery store of the family of **Clementine Poto Langone** (1898-1964) is now a coffee shop. As a child, she helped pack Italian food products to send west to Italian immigrants working on the transcontinental railroads. The grocery store was on the first floor with living quarters upstairs. When Clementine married Joseph Langone Jr. in 1920, she moved next door to 190 North Street. In the 1930s, after her husband was elected to public office, she helped many Italian immigrants become citizens so they could be eligible for social security benefits and provided food and clothing to Italian people out of work. She was an active member of the North End Union.

N6: Home of Rachel and Paul Revere; Rachel Revere Park

19 North Square

When she became **Rachel Walker Revere** (1745-1813) by marrying the recently-widowed Paul Revere in 1773, Rachel took on the care of the six surviving children born to Paul's first wife, **Sarah Orne Revere** (1736-73), who died four months after her eighth child was born. Rachel had eight more children, three of whom did not reach maturity. Large families and a high infant mortality rate were common during colonial times. In 1775, Rachel held the family and business together when the British did not allow Revere to return to Boston after his famous ride. She eventually joined him in Watertown until they returned to their home after the British evacuated Boston on March 17, 1776. Across the street is **Rachel Revere Park**, first dedicated in 1946 and restored at the time of the Bicentennial in July 1976.

Rachel Revere

"My dear Doctr Church I send a hundred & twenty five pounds and beg you will take the best care of your self and not attempt coming in to this town again and if I have an opportunity of coming or sending out any thing or any of the Children I shall do it."
—Rachel Revere to Dr. Benjamin Church, ca. April 18, 1775, trying to send help to her husband, Paul, who was captured the next day by the British

Revere
House,
interior

N7: Mariners House

11 North Square

Sarah Josepha Hale (1788-1879), editor of *Boston's Ladies' Magazine*, established the Seaman's Aid Society in 1833 to provide employment for the wives of sailors as seamstresses and a place to sell their work. The Society also opened a Mariners House in the North End as a sailors' boarding house and developed an industrial school for seamen's daughters and a day nursery. Hale later became the editor of *Godey's Lady's Book*. In September of 1840, Hale organized the great women's fair which raised enough money to complete the Bunker Hill monument. It had stood unfinished for more than a decade (see D17).

☞ *Directions: Continue straight through North Square to Garden Court.*

A woman's "...first right is to education in its widest sense, to such education as will give her the full development of all her personal, mental and moral qualities." —Sarah Josepha Hale

N8: Rose Fitzgerald Kennedy Birthplace

4 Garden Court

The birthplace of **Rose Fitzgerald Kennedy** (1890-1995) was probably a bow fronted building like the one at No. 6 Garden Court. She was the first child of six born to **Josephine Hannon** and John F. Fitzgerald, who became Democratic boss of the North End's Ward six and a leading Catholic spokesman for the Irish community, before being elected mayor in 1905. For Rose Kennedy's life, see N1.

☞ *Directions: Continue along Garden Court to Fleet Street. Turn left to Hanover Street.*

 Sarah Josepha Hale

N9: Universalist Meeting House

332 Hanover Street (now the North End Community Center)

Writer **Judith Sargent Murray** (1751-1820), an advocate for women's equality, attended Boston's first Universalist church at this site when she moved to Boston in 1794 (see D24). Her husband, Reverend John Murray, an early Universalist minister, held the church's pulpit from 1793 until 1809 when he suffered a stroke. Among the progressive ideas preached here was the equality of male and female souls—not unlike views espoused years earlier by **Anne Hutchinson** (see D1) and **Mary Dyer** (see

Universalist Meeting House

D2). In her writing, Murray used her theological knowledge to challenge the legitimacy of the centuries-old "Fall of Eve" myth and its damaging effect on views about women.

☞ *Directions: Turn right on Hanover Street.*

N10: Old St. Stephen's Church

401 Hanover Street
The only remaining church in Boston designed by architect Charles Bulfinch was completed in 1804. Its history reflects the neighborhood. In 1862, it became a Roman Catholic Church and **Rose Fitzgerald Kennedy** and her father were christened here. On the pews are the names of the North End women and men who helped raise the funds for the church's restoration in 1965. A marker in memory of Rose Kennedy commemorates her baptism (see N1 and N8).

"As I look back upon [my] life, it seems to me that it would have been impossible for me to have led any other... To be thoroughly in earnest, intensely in earnest in all my thoughts and in all my actions, whether in my profession or out of it, became my one single idea. And I honestly believe herein lies the secret of my success in life. I do not believe that any great success in any art can be achieved without it...."
—Charlotte Cushman

☞ *Directions: Cross Hanover Street. Enter Revere Mall.*

N11: Plaques to North End Women

Revere Mall
Three women prominent in North End history are honored by plaques on the left wall of Revere Mall. At the age of ten, **Ann Pollard** (1620-1725) was probably the first white woman to come ashore in Boston, landing with Governor John Winthrop at the foot of today's Prince Street. **Dr. Harriot Keziah Hunt** (1805-75), who grew up on the waterfront at the foot of Hanover Street, became a doctor through self-study after being refused permission to attend lectures at Harvard Medical School. A women's rights advocate and social reformer, Hunt advocated health education for women. **Charlotte Cushman** (1816-76), who was born on the site of the present North End branch library, became an internationally-known actress renowned for playing both male and female roles. She established a salon in Rome for women sculptors including Boston sculptors **Anne Whitney** (see B15) and **Edmonia Lewis** (see D10) and Watertown's **Harriet Hosmer**.

Charlotte Cushman

Members of the Saturday Evening Girls' Club and associated Library Clubs decorating pieces of Paul Revere Pottery at 18 Hull Street, ca. 1912

Samples of the highly collectible pottery

☞ *Directions: Walk past the Old North Church and St. Francis of Assisi Garden to Salem Street. Cross to Hull Street.*

N12: Paul Revere Pottery and Library Clubhouse

18 Hull Street
The first home of the Paul Revere Pottery, founded in 1908 by librarian **Edith Guerrier** (1870-1958) and artist **Edith Brown** (1872-1932) and funded by philanthropist **Helen Osborne Storrow** (1864-1944), was in the basement of this building. Reflecting the philosophy of the Arts and Crafts Movement, the pottery provided worthwhile employment for young North End Italian and Jewish women. The lower floors of the building served as the Library Club House under the supervision of Guerrier, where

young women formed clubs for reading, storytelling, and dramatics named for their meeting times. The **Saturday Evening Girls** continued to meet until 1969. Many of the Saturday Evening Girls went on to careers in teaching and business. One of the most distinguished was **Fanny Goldstein** (1888-1961), who became the curator of Judaica for the Boston Public Library.

The Pottery moved to Nottingham Hill in Brighton in 1915, operating until 1942.

☞ *Directions: Return to Salem Street and turn right.*

N13: North Bennet Street Industrial School

Corner of Salem and North Bennet Streets
Pauline Agassiz Shaw (1841-1917) founded the **North Bennet Street Industrial School** in 1881 to train newly arrived Italian and Jewish people in skilled trades. America's first trade school, the school now holds an international reputation for courses in fine furniture, jewelry, violin making, carpentry, and piano and violin restoration. Shaw, active in social reform, gave financial support to the woman suffrage movement. She is also responsible for the institutionalization of kindergartens in Boston Public Schools.

Pauline Agassiz Shaw

moved to Dorchester in 1936 where it served the community for another thirty years, becoming a home for orphan Jewish children and then a full service community center for the Jewish and then the changing Dorchester-Roxbury-Mattapan community. The Hecht Neighborhood House merged with Young Men's Hebrew Association (YMHA) of Boston in 1958/59 to become YMHA-Hecht House.

☞ *Directions: Return to Prince Street and turn right. Turn left on Hanover Street.*

In the 1880s, she developed kindergartens in fourteen schools using her own funds and energy. In 1887, the School Committee accepted responsibility for continuing those kindergartens, gradually adding more. Today, one of Boston's public schools in Dorchester is named for her.

☞ *Directions: Walk down Salem Street and cross Prince Street to Baldwin Place on the right.*

N14: Hebrew Industrial School
Baldwin Place
One of the locations of the Hebrew Industrial School, founded for girls in 1889, was near the North Bennet Street Industrial School. It was later named for Jewish activist **Lina Hecht** (1848-1920). At a time when nearly a third of the North End's population was Jewish, the school was established to train Jewish women in needlework skills. Anxious to teach their own youth, the Hebrew Ladies' Sewing Society donated cloth and sewing machines for classes in millinery, hand sewing, power sewing, and pattern cutting. The school became Hecht Neighborhood House in 1922 in a different place and

Lina Hecht

N15: St. Leonard's Church
Hanover Street, between North Bennet and Prince Streets
St. Leonard's Church was the first Roman Catholic Church founded by Italian immigrants in Boston. Built in 1873, St. Leonard's was restored in 1988. Women were prominent in the drive which raised more than a million dollars for the project. Their names are included on the tablets in the church's Peace Garden.

☞ *Directions: Turn back down Hanover Street and walk to the Rose Kennedy Greenway.*

End of Walk

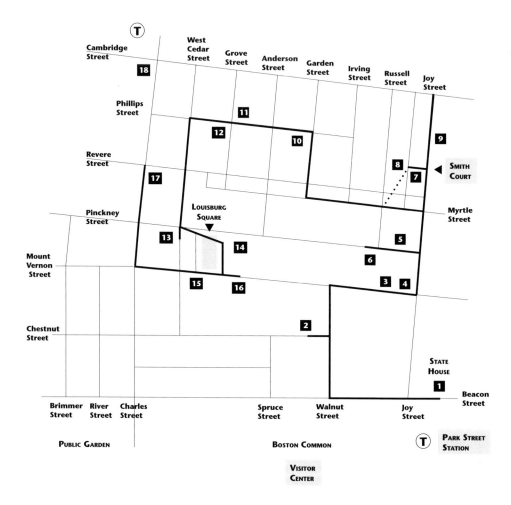

Beacon Hill Walk

Use this map for all "B" sites

(T) = MBTA stop

(M) = historic marker

Beacon Hill Walk

"Activists, Artists, Dissenters, and Writers"

The Beacon Hill Walk begins at the Massachusetts State House with the statues of two seventeenth century women religious dissenters. The walk continues up, down, and across Beacon Hill, often paralleling the Black Heritage Trail. Starting with intense activity in the period before and after the Civil War and continuing into the nineteenth century, women writers and artists living here supported social movements ranging from anti-slavery to suffrage. The walk pays particular attention to the story of Beacon Hill's African American women and of Boston's first women doctors and professional nurses. Beacon Hill is a designated Historic District with narrow, steep, sometimes cobblestone streets, and brick homes featuring beautiful doorways and window boxes. It was first developed by the Mount Vernon Proprietors in 1795. Charles Street along its western edge includes antique and specialty shops, restaurants, and grocery stores.

Time: 1 1/2 hours
Begins: Massachusetts State House
☞ **Directions:** Go to the statue of Mary Dyer in front of the East Wing.

B1: Statues of Women Dissenters: Mary Dyer and Anne Hutchinson

State House, fronting the East and West Wings
Two of Boston's earliest dissenters were **Mary Dyer** (d. 1660) and **Anne Hutchinson** (1591-1643). Mary Dyer, a Quaker, witnessed on the Boston Common two times before she was hung for heresy. Anne Hutchinson was banished from Boston after she accused the Puritan oligarchy of preaching that "good works" would bring God's grace. As a pledge of their friendship and shared belief in the role of religious dissenters, Mary Dyer walked beside Hutchinson after she was excommunicated from the Puritan church. (For more details on their stories, see D1, 2.)

☞ *Directions: Continue down Beacon Street to Walnut Street. Turn right. At Chestnut Street, turn left.*

B2: Hepzibah Clarke Swan and Julia Ward Howe

13-17 Chestnut Street
Designed by Charles Bulfinch ca. 1806, this house represents the lives of two notable Boston women: **Hepzibah Clarke Swan** (1757-1825) and **Julia Ward Howe** (1819-1910). Swan was one of

The houses owned by Hepzibah Clarke Swan

the five original members of the Mount Vernon proprietors whose goal was to transform Beacon Hill into a fashionable neighborhood. At the time it was rare for a woman to own property in her own name. Possessing inherited wealth, she married James Swan who lost a great deal of her fortune before she divorced him. She built the three row houses at numbers 13, 15, 17 for her daughters and another for herself at number 16. Her collection of French furnishings is now in the Boston Museum of Fine Arts, as are several of the family portraits she commissioned Gilbert Stuart to paint.

"It is a new world today. I find it filled with a new hope and brightened by a new inspiration."
—Julia Ward Howe

Julia Ward Howe

Julia Ward Howe, who is best known as the author of *The Battle Hymn of the Republic* written at the beginning of the Civil War, lived at 13 Chestnut during that period, one of her several residences in Boston. Howe was a noted reformer and early participant in the women's club movement after the war. She was joined by a group of women, including **Caroline Severance** (1820-1914), in founding the New England Women's Club in 1868, one of the first women's clubs in the country. She followed Severance as president. Howe was a leader in the woman suffrage movement and helped found the *Woman's Journal*. Howe read papers at the meetings of the Radical Club, a club for women and

men who were "daring thinkers" which often met at this site. In 1879, three years after her husband's death, she moved to 241 Beacon Street (see BBE12).

☞ *Directions: Return to Walnut Street and turn left. Turn right on Mount Vernon Street.*

Rose Nichols

B3: Rose Nichols and Nichols House Museum
55 Mount Vernon Street
Rose Standish Nichols (1872-1964) was among the first well-known women landscape architects and a lifelong pacifist who lived on Mount Vernon Street her entire life. She traveled extensively throughout the world and developed an interest in international politics. She left her house to the public and as a place for offices of organizations promoting international friendship.

☞ *Directions: Continue up Mount Vernon Street.*

B4: Portia School of Law
45-47 Mount Vernon Street
Portia School of Law began in 1908 when two women who wanted to take the Massachusetts bar examination asked Attorney Arthur W. MacLean to tutor them. His wife, **Bertha MacLean**, named the nascent school after "Portia" who disguises herself as a lawyer in

Shakespeare's *Merchant of Venice*. The informal school expanded and became the only school providing legal education for women exclusively. Portia Law was incorporated in 1919 and in 1920 the first L.L.B. degrees were awarded to thirty-nine women. The school continued to grow, admitting a few men in 1930. The first woman dean was **Margaret H. Bauer** (1899-1985), who served in various capacities at the school from 1937 until 1962, becoming dean in 1952. In June 1972, the name of the school was changed to the New England School of Law. It moved to 154 Stuart Street in 1980.

In 1923, **Blanche Woodson Braxton** (1894-1939), a graduate of Portia Law in 1921, became the first African American woman to be admitted to the Massachusetts Bar. She later became the first African American woman admitted to practice in the U.S. District Court in the state. The first woman president of the Board of Trustees of New England School of Law was **Anna E. Hirsch** (1902-97), a 1928 graduate of Portia Law. Hirsch was elected register of probate for Norfolk County in 1954 and 1960 (see also C2).

A 1940s class in legal history

"I am prepared to certify that she has studied law for two years in a law school identical as to curriculum and methods with the Harvard Law School." —Joseph Beale, Harvard Law School, supporting a student's application to the Bar in 1918.

☞ *Directions: Turn left on Joy Street. Turn left on Pinckney Street.*

"My mother said, 'Every child should be taught as if he or she were a genius.'" —Elizabeth Peabody

Elizabeth Peabody

B5: Elizabeth Peabody's Kindergarten
15 Pinckney Street
One of the locations for the kindergarten of **Elizabeth Palmer Peabody** (1804-94) (see C1), considered the founder of the kindergarten movement in the United States, was at 15 Pinckney Street which, although destroyed, was the mirror image of 17 Pinckney Street. Influenced by the ideas of Friedrich Fröebel, Peabody became an advocate for kindergartens nationwide, publishing the *Kindergarten Messenger* and organizing the American Froebel Union. She was a link between the visionaries of the Transcendental movement and educational reformerss.

B6: Home of Louisa May Alcott
20 Pinckney Street
Although author **Louisa May Alcott** (1832-88) is best known for her book, *Little Women*, describing her family life in Concord, Massachusetts, she had several Boston homes. The daughter of famed Transcendentalist Bronson Alcott, she lived here in rented rooms as a child. As an adult, she often stayed with other

Louisa May Alcott

"So hard to move people out of old ruts. I haven't patience enough. If they won't see and work, I let 'em alone and steam along my own way."
—Louisa May Alcott

reformist women in the "sky parlor" of the Bellevue Hotel on Beacon Street, owned by Dr. Dio Lewis, principal of Boston's Normal Institute for Physical Education, and near her publisher, Roberts Brothers. In the last decade of her life, Alcott purchased a home for her family at 10 Louisburg Square, but was too ill to enjoy it for herself. She died at the age of 55, probably of poison from the mercury used to treat the typhoid fever she contracted as a Civil War nurse (see D4 and SE19).

African Meeting House

☞ *Directions: Return to Joy Street and turn left to the corner of Smith Court.*

B7: Museum of African American History and Abiel Smith School
46 Joy Street
The Museum of African American History, which was founded in 1964 by **Sue Bailey Thurman** (1903-96), acquired the neighboring African Meeting House in 1972. Among its former directors was **Ruth Batson** (1921-2003), a leading civil rights activist in Boston. She was chairperson of the education committee of the Boston NAACP that led the fight in the early 1960s against segregation in the Boston Public Schools and a founder and later director of the METCO voluntary desegregation program.

The Abiel Smith School served African American children from 1835 to 1855 until the state legislature passed an act allowing them to attend the school closest to their homes. The change was prompted by the actions of Benjamin Roberts, an African American, who sued the city in 1848 stating that his daughter **Sarah Roberts** was unlawfully refused entrance to five schools between her home and the Smith School. Although Roberts lost his case despite the help of prominent abolitionists, his actions had the long term effect of opening all Boston Public Schools to African American children.

☞ *Directions: Enter Smith Court.*

B8: African Meeting House
8 Smith Court
The church, the oldest standing African American church building in America, was built in 1805-6 in the heart of Boston's Afrcan American community on the north slope of Beacon Hill.

Among women abolitionists active in this church before the Civil War was **Maria Stewart** (1803-79) who challenged other free African American women: "O, ye daughters of Africa, Awake! Awake! Arise! No longer sleep nor slumber, but distinguish yourselves. Show forth to the world that ye are endowed with noble and exalted faculties." Stewart is credited as the first American-born woman to speak in public before an audience that included both men and women.

Susan Paul (see also B13), whose father was the minister, joined other African American women to form a temperance society in the 1830s. William Lloyd Garrison founded the New England Anti-Slavery society here in 1832 and the church became a center for abolitionist activity. Escaped slaves William and **Ellen Craft** (1826-97) were active in abolition meetings here (see B12).

☞ *Directions: Return to Joy Street. Turn left.*

B9: Home of Rebecca Lee Crumpler

67 Joy Street

Dr. Rebecca Lee Crumpler (1831-95) is considered to be the first African American woman doctor. She received a "Doctress of Medicine" in 1864 from the New England Female Medical College in Boston's South End, later merged into the Boston University School of Medicine. Born in Delaware, Crumpler was raised in Pennsylvania by an aunt. She came to Charlestown in 1852 where she worked as a nurse. After she received her degree, she practiced in post Civil War Virginia. With her husband, Dr. Arthur Crumpler, she next moved back to Boston where she set up her medical practice on Joy Street. She focused on women and children and emphasized nutrition and preventive medicine. She pulled together her experiences and knowledge in *A Book of Medical Discourses in Two Parts.*

☞ *Directions: Continue down Joy Street to 81 Joy to find the marker locating the home of* **Maria Stewart***, then called 8 Belknap Street (see B8).*

Return to the African Meeting House. Go to the end of Smith Court, turn left to follow the narrow public way to Russell Street. Continue up to Myrtle Street. An alternative is to go back up Joy Street to Myrtle Street. For either route, turn right on Myrtle Street. Pass the former Bowdoin School, which in the 1890s and longer, was a Boston public grammar school for girls. Turn right on Garden Street to Phillips Street and turn left.

B10: The Vilna Shul

14-18 Phillips Street

The Vilna Shul was built in 1919 to serve the Jewish community on Beacon Hill as a synagogue and community center. Although it closed in 1985, the building has been restored as a Jewish cultural center. Before they built the synagogue, the congregation of Lithuanian Jews worshipped in temporary spaces for nearly twenty-five years. They named the synagogue for the city of Vilnius, because

Interior of the Vilna Shul

they considered it to be the center of Jewish culture in Lithuania. Many of the original members of the congregation emigrated from Vilnius where there was a large and thriving Jewish community. Only a few decades later it was destroyed by the Holocaust.

The names of the women who were among the founding members of the synagogue are listed in a plaque in the back of the sanctuary. Although the entire congregation sat on the same level, the women's section was separate from the men's section but equal in size (which was typical of synagogues of that time). The Vilna Shul is also a significant site because it represents the large Jewish community who made their first Boston homes in the old West End and on the north slope of Beacon Hill.

☞ *Directions: Continue on Phillips Street.*

B11: View of Massachusetts General Hospital, Linda Richards and Mary Eliza Mahoney

(from corner of Phillips and Grove Streets)
Linda Richards (1841-1930) pioneered professional nurses' training at Massachusetts General Hospital. In 1873 she had received the first diploma from the country's first nursing school which was organized at the New England Hospital for Women and Children. The hospital, founded in Roxbury in 1863 and run by **Dr. Marie Zakrzewska** (1829-1902) and a board of women reformers, is now the

Linda Richards

Dimock Community Health Center (see SE21). The Palmer-Davis Library at Massachusetts General is named for **Sophia Palmer** (1853-1920) and **Mary E. P. Davis** (1840-1924), both students of Linda Richards. Palmer and Davis co-founded the *American Journal of Nursing* and created the American Nurses Association by bringing together alumnae associations of nurses' training schools.

Mary Eliza Mahoney

Mary Eliza Mahoney (1845-1926), the first African American woman to become a registered nurse, also graduated from the New England Hospital. Mahoney is honored by a medal awarded annually by the American Nurses Association. **Mary Vincent** (1818-87) was an actress whose friends funded the Vincent Memorial Hospital, part of Massachusetts General, in her memory in 1891. The women of the Vincent Club continue to raise money by producing an annual theatrical show. The hospital pioneered in women's health, including the development of the "Pap Smear."

☞ *Directions: Continue on Phillips Street.*

"It was my determination to...create a good foundation of respect for women physicians." —Dr. Marie Zakrzewska

Ellen Craft, in disguise

"I had rather starve in England, a free woman, than be a slave for the best man that ever breathed on American soil."
—Ellen Craft

B12: Hayden House, Ellen and William Craft

66 Phillips Street

This station on the Underground Railroad was a destination for many fugitive slaves, including **Ellen Craft** (1826-97) and her husband, William. In 1848 she disguised herself as her master, bandaged as if ill, and tended to by her husband as if he were the slave. They escaped from Georgia by taking the train and steamer to Boston. After two years in Boston where they were active in the anti-slavery cause, they sailed to England, staying until after the Civil War because the new Fugitive Slave Law endangered their lives. **Harriet Hayden** (ca. 1816-93) and her husband, Lewis Hayden, both born slaves, owned this house for more than forty years. They worked with Underground Railroad "conductor" **Harriet Tubman** (ca. 1820-1913), known as the "Moses of her People," in moving slaves to safe havens (see SE5, 6). Harriet Hayden bequeathed a scholarship for "needy and worthy colored students" at Harvard Medical School.

☞ *Directions: Continue along Phillips Street. Turn left on West Cedar Street, Cross Pinckney Street.*

B13: Home of Susan Paul

36 West Cedar Street

In the 1830s, **Susan Paul** (1809-41) taught at the Smith School on Joy Street, a segregated school for African American children funded jointly by the city and private donations (see B7). Paul was also an officer in the Boston Female Anti-Slavery Society founded by **Maria Weston Chapman** in 1832 (see D24). She was the daughter of Thomas Paul, the founder of the African Baptist Church, and supported her mother after his death. Some of her letters were printed in William Lloyd Garrison's *Liberator*. In 1834 she wrote to condemn the "spirit which persecutes us on account of our color—that cruel prejudice which deprives us of every privilege whereby we might elevate ourselves—and then condemns us because we are not more refined and intelligent."

☞ *Directions: Return to Pinckney Street. Turn right and walk up to Louisburg Square.*

B14: St. Margaret's Convent

19 Louisburg Square

Originally founded in Sussex, England, in 1855 to care for the poor and ill in the surrounding countryside, this Episcopalian religious community came to Boston in 1873 to act as superintendents of a children's hospital. The sisters moved to

Interior of St. Margaret's Convent in 1990

three townhouses on Louisburg Square in 1883 which they used as a convent, chapel, and small hospital. Here, they expanded their nursing and evangelical teachings to reach the sick and poor on Beacon Hill and its environs. They ran St. Monica's Home, a nursing home for Black women and children, on Joy Street and later in Roxbury until 1988. In 1992, the St. Margaret's community moved the Motherhouse to Roxbury.

☞ *Directions: Walk through Louisburg Square to Mount Vernon Street. On your way, note 10 Louisburg Square, the last residence of* **Louisa May Alcott**.

Anne Whitney (seated) with Adeline Manning

B15: Anne Whitney Studio
92 Mount Vernon Street
The window on the top of this building marked the studio for two decades of sculptor **Anne Whitney** (1821-1915), who was part of a group of American women sculptors gathering around actress **Charlotte Cushman** (see N11) in Rome in the mid-nineteenth century. In 1873, soon after Whitney returned to Boston, she received a commission for the statue of Sam Adams now standing outside Faneuil Hall. Her statue of Leif Eriksson is on the Commonwealth Avenue Mall (see BBE1, BBW21). Her bust of **Lucy Stone** is in the Boston Public Library (see BBW1), and her sculpture of abolitionist William

Lloyd Garrison is in the Massachusetts Historical Society. Whitney had a "Boston marriage" with her longtime partner **Adeline Manning**. During the late Victorian era, such marriages between women, generally professional and upper class, were both common and accepted by society at large.

☞ *Directions: Continue up Mount Vernon Street.*

B16: Home of Margaret Deland
76 Mount Vernon Street
Margaret Deland (1857-1945) was a popular novelist at the turn of the twentieth century and a social reformer. Her twenty-five works of fiction were set both in historical and modern times and dealt with making ethical decisions in different settings. Although she considered herself a "new woman" determined to preserve her freedom of action, she did not support woman suffrage. Her charity was personal; she took young unwed mothers into her home until they could become self-supporting, believing that their love for their babies would provide an incentive.

☞ *Directions: Turn around and go down Mount Vernon Street to Charles Street. Turn right.*

B17: Josephine St. Pierre Ruffin, Florida Ruffin Ridley, and The Woman's Era Club
103 Charles Street
Josephine St. Pierre Ruffin (1842-1924), African American editor and publisher of *The Woman's Era*, the journal of the New Era Club, lived here for two decades (see SE18). She founded the club for African American women in 1894. A year later,

"For the sake of ...the dignity of our race, and future good name of our children, it is... our duty to stand forth and declare our principles."
—Josephine St. Pierre Ruffin

Josephine St. P. Ruffin

she organized a national conference to form the National Federation of Afro-American Women to show the existence of a "large and growing class" of cultured African American women. They met at the Charles Street A.M.E. Church (now Charles Street Meeting House) and merged with the Colored Women's League to form the National Association of Colored Women in 1896. Ruffin served as the first vice president. Although it was accepted by the Massachusetts State Federation of Womens' Clubs, the New Era Club was refused membership in the national federation in 1900 for fear of offending Southern members. Her husband, George Lewis Ruffin, was Boston's first African American municipal judge.

Florida Ruffin Ridley (1861-1943), Ruffin's daughter, became the second African American teacher in the Boston Public Schools. She was active with her mother in the New Era Club as well as in the League of Women for Community Service. She also became a member of several predominantly white clubs, including the Twentieth Century Club and the Women's City Club of Boston. In addition to her work as a club woman and civil rights activist, Ridley was an essayist and journalist, focusing much of her writing on race relations in New England. In the 1920s, her interest in

history led her to found the Society of the Descendants of Early New England Negroes. Through this work, she hoped to connect an understanding of history with contemporary work for social justice. African Americans and whites have always been involved, she wrote, "in the eternal war for justice and liberty which the state has waged." Then, as in her own time, she believed both races deserved an equal place in society.

☞ *Directions: Look right to the end of Charles Street.*

B18: Annie Adams Fields (view site)
148 Charles Street
Although the home of **Annie Adams Fields** (1834-1915) and her husband, publisher James T. Fields, at the end of Charles Street, does not survive, it was the site of their important literary salon (see D6, 19). After his death in 1881, Annie Fields continued to support the work of many women writers, including **Sarah Orne Jewett** (1849-1909) who spent winters with her, poet **Louise Imogen Guiney** (see BBW1), and **Harriet Beecher Stowe** (1811-96). Fields was also active in charitable works. She spent many hours at the Charity House on Chardon Street and cofounded the Cooperative Society of Visitors, a case review agency that made recommendations to the central administration of Boston's relief organizations for aid disbursement. The Society was absorbed into the Associated Charities of Boston. Fields's book *How to Help the Poor* (1884) served as an unofficial guide to the programs and policies of Associated Charities.

☞ *Directions: Turn back down Charles Street to Beacon Street and the Public Garden.*

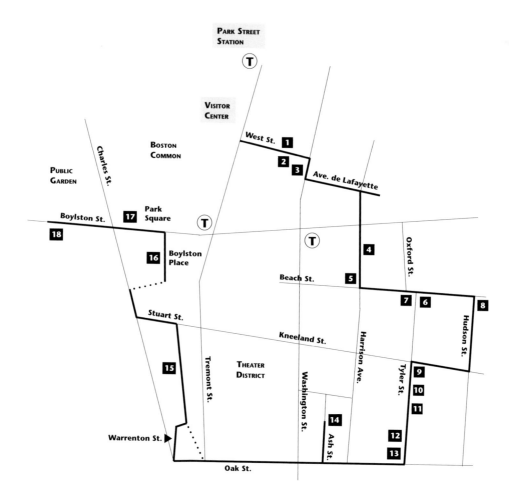

South Cove/Chinatown Walk

Use this map for all "C" sites

(T) = MBTA stop

(M) = historic marker

Chinatown/South Cove Walk

"Action for Social and Economic Justice"

The Chinatown/South Cove Walk starts at the Visitor Center on
Boston Common, winds through Chinatown, and ends at Park Square.
It presents a wide range of women's activities and organizations working for social
change and economic justice. The focus is on immigrant groups, most recently Chinese.
The walk also includes a women's settlement house serving an earlier immigrant
population, and the international programs of a Catholic sisterhood.

The South Cove area, originally the South Cove of Boston Harbor, was
filled in between 1833-39. Beach Street takes its name from its former location
along the edge of the harbor. Although the Chinese community began arriving in
the mid-nineteenth century, large numbers of women were not allowed until
the liberalization of immigration laws in the mid-twentieth century.
The people of the Chinese community give the area its special spirit,
along with its architecture, murals, restaurants, groceries, and shops.

Time: 1 1/2 hours
Begins: Visitor Welcome Center, Boston Common
☞ **Directions:** From the Visitor Center, cross Tremont Street, turn down West Street.

C1: Elizabeth Peabody Book Shop

13-15 West Street
The Book Shop of **Elizabeth Peabody**
(1804-94) is best known as the location
of the 1839-44 Conversations led by
Margaret Fuller (1810-50) which
helped crystallize New England
Transcendentalism, a movement
encouraging the perfection of each
individual. A regular participant in these
Conversations was philosopher and activist
Ednah Dow Littlehale Cheney (1824-
1904) who, at age 16, was the youngest
participant (see also BBW8). Fuller

Margaret Fuller

*"We only ask of men to remove arbitrary barriers....But if you ask me what offices they may
fill, I reply — any. I do not care what case you put; let them be sea captains if you will.
I do not doubt there are women well fitted for such an office."* —Margaret Fuller, 1845

received an intense classical education from her father and became known as an intellectual prodigy. Working with Ralph Waldo Emerson and others, she edited the transcendentalist journal *The Dial* and was the first woman journalist for the *New York Tribune*. Her essay *Woman in the Nineteenth Century* is an American feminist classic.

Elizabeth Peabody, who was also a Transcendentalist, founded American kindergartens (see B5) and here at the Book Shop became the first woman publisher in Boston. Her younger sisters were each married in the family parlor behind the Book Shop. **Sophia Peabody** (1809-71), an artist, married author **Nathaniel Hawthorne**, and **Mary Peabody** (1806-87), an educator, married **Horace Mann**, considered to be the father of American public education.

C2: Massachusetts Bar Association

20 West Street
The first woman member of the Massachusetts Bar Association was **Mary A. Mahan** of West Roxbury, who was admitted in 1913. Many women lawyers in Boston attended Portia School of Law, established in 1908 (see B4). After Mahan was admitted along with with thirty-four men, a member spoke up saying he hoped her admission would "not interfere with our banquets and prevent smoking," but, he added, showing his pride in their action, "the question of women members has been brought before the American Bar Association and the members have dodged it."

☞ *Directions: Turn right on Washington Street.*

C3: Sarah Caldwell and the Boston Opera House

539 Washington Street
As founder of The Opera Company, **Sarah Caldwell** (1924-2006) staged and conducted full-fledged performances of operas at various venues in Boston from 1957 to 1991. In 1980 the Opera Company acquired The Opera House. With her compelling and demanding personality, Caldwell charted a new course for opera in America. She had a special talent for producing flamboyant theatrical effects and with her adventurous spirit she embraced the whole spectrum of operatic possibilities. In 1976 she became the first woman to conduct at the Metropolitan Opera House. She received thirty-five honorary degrees and in 1997 the National Medal of the Arts (see SE32).

☞ *Directions: Turn left on Avenue de Lafayette and right on Harrison Avenue Extension to Harrison Avenue.*

C4: Telephone Exchange

2-8 Harrison Avenue and Oxford Place
A successful and nonviolent strike of 8,000 women telephone operators in April 1919, led by **Julia O'Connor [Parker]** (1890-1972), paralyzed telephone service in five New England states for six days. This building is an expansion of the Oxford

Women telephone operators on strike in 1919

A woman telephone operator at new England Telephone, ca. 1926

of fifty-two hours), and an increased minimum wage. Today UNITE represents the Union of Needle Industrial and Textile Employees.

☞ *Directions: Turn left on Beach Street. Cross Beach Street to Tyler Street. South and east of Beach Street was South Cove, a tidal flat until the 1830s.*

Street exchange where O'Connor worked. Switchboard operators, who were mostly young, single Irish-American women, were expected to work at breakneck speed often on split shifts. They were punished with detention as if they were still in high school. Supported by the Women's Trade Union League, O'Connor and her team negotiated a settlement that included a $3 to $4 weekly raise (see C16). Starting in 1939, she worked for eighteen years as an organizer for the AFL.

Chew Shee Chin

C5: International Ladies Garment Workers Union (ILGWU), present office of UNITE

31 Harrison Avenue
Although only a few clothing factories still operate in this area, Harrison and Kneeland streets were once the center of the New England ready-made clothing industry. The WPA Federal Writers' Guide said that on "warm days the hum of hundreds of sewing machines can be heard through the open windows." In 1936, the winter after the National Labor Relations Act gave workers the right to organize, hundreds of women garment workers joined a strike supported by the ILGWU and the Amalgamated Clothing Workers that lasted two months. In April they won a closed shop, a forty-hour week (instead

C6: New England Chinese Women's Association

2 Tyler Street
The New England Chinese Women's Association was founded in 1942 by **Chew Shee Chin** (1899-1985) and other Boston Chinese women in response to **Madame Chiang Kai Shek's** appeal for China relief during World War II. The association continues to serve the Boston Chinese community as a networking and social service organization. Chew Shee Chin was one of the first Chinese-American women to work in Boston's garment industry (see C5).

C7: Phillis Wheatley Landing Place

Beach and Tyler Streets
Phillis Wheatley (ca. 1753-84), the first published African American woman poet

in America, landed while still a small child in 1761 in the slave ship *Phillis* at Avery's Wharf located near the present position of Tyler Street. She was purchased at auction by the Wheatley family. Her mistress, **Suzannah Wheatley** (d. 1774) became her mentor (see also D21). Phillis Wheatley is one of three women chosen to be portrayed in the Boston Women's Memorial (see BBW23).

☞ *Directions: Cross to Beach Street to Oxford Place. Take an immediate left into the vest pocket park to view the four-story mural, "Travellers in an Autumn Landscape," painted by Wang Yun (1652-1735) with ink on silk and owned by the Museum of Fine Arts. This Chinatown Heritage Mural was created by Wen-ti Tsen and Yuon Zuo. Return to Beach Street and turn left. Walk through the arch and turn right to the Chinatown Gateway Park on Hudson Street and the Rose Kennedy Greenway (see N1).*

FOO
Continued from the First Page

The thrice-married Mrs. Foo was one of Boston's most well-known figures for many years. Besides her famed "Den" on

RUBY FOO

Hudson st., she owned a part interest in a New York "Den." Her elaborate Chinese restaurant here was known throughout the country and leading theatrical and sports figures flocked to taste the Chinese specialties.

Ruby Foo's obituary in the *Boston Daily Globe*

C8: Ruby Foo's Den
Beach and Hudson Streets
Born in San Francisco, **Ruby Foo** (1904-50) moved to Boston in 1923 where she began a single-room restaurant in Boston's Chinatown. Its popularity quickly grew, and she opened Ruby Foo's "Den" on Hudson Street in 1929—heralded as the first Chinese restaurant to successfully cater to non-Chinese clientele. Throughout World War II, the Den remained a legendary meeting place for theatrical and sports figures and other celebrities. She opened similar restaurants in New York, Miami, Washington and Providence, becoming a nationally-known restaurateur and mentor to dozens of aspiring chefs in her native Boston. In 1938, newspapers ran a photo of a Chinese baby sitting amidst rubble in a Shanghai railroad station that had been bombed by the Japanese. Foo had the child brought to the United States where she adopted him and raised him along with her other children.

☞ *Directions: Before leaving Gateway Park, note the Tianamin Memorial dedicated in 1989 to honor the 1989 Democracy Movement in China. Walk south along Hudson to Kneeland Street. Turn right. Turn left on Tyler Street.*

C9: Hannah Shakir and the Lebanese-Syrian Ladies' Aid Society
76 Tyler Street
Among the founders of the Lebanese-Syrian Ladies' Aid Society was **Hannah Sabbagh Shakir** (1895-1990) who emigrated from Lebanon with her family to the South End in 1907 when she was twelve. In 1917, she joined other women to form the society so they could raise money to send clothes, blankets, and money to contacts in Lebanon.

Their fundraising events, including plays showcasing Arab classics, made them a center for the social life of their community. They continued to provide relief for new arrivals and during World War II for people in the Near East. The society later moved to the South End (see SE24).

Hannah Shakir worked as a stitcher in a Boston textile factory as a young woman. In 1944 she opened her own textile factory, Parkway Manufacturing, in West Roxbury which employed fifteen people to make women's clothing. It continued in business for thirty years.

Mother Mary
Joseph Rogers

C10: Maryknoll Sisters

79 Tyler Street

Mother Mary Joseph Rogers (1882-1955), a Boston Public School graduate and teacher, founded the Maryknoll Sisters of St. Dominic, a national order whose members were first known for their professional service in China before the Communist takeover. Rogers insisted that the sisters be trained professionally for their missionary work and that they work together as equals, sharing all household tasks. Under her leadership, over 1,000 women worked throughout the world in over twenty-five different countries spreading their message of Justice, Love

and Peace in God's name, and living with and caring for those in need. The sisters still serve all over the world today, particularly in Latin America. The mission on Tyler Street served the Chinese community until 1992.

C11: Quincy School

90 Tyler Street

When the innovative Quincy School opened in 1847, teachers had their own classrooms for the first time in America. Women teachers were in charge of each grade, but were supervised by a male principal. Students sat at their own desks instead of at long benches. Boys and girls attended different grammar schools; the Quincy School was for boys.

In 1905, the Quincy school district employed Boston's first school nurse, **Annie McKay** (1867-1944), after the School Committee authorized the Visiting Nurse Association to select and supervise a school nurse. In her first eight weeks, McKay saw 125 cases in schools and made 576 home visits. Her work had such positive results with reducing absenteeism and exclusion that within two years, the school committee had authorized the hiring of thirty-three more nurses to service Boston elementary schools and the state had mandated at least one doctor and school nurse in every school system.

Today, the Chinese-American Civic Association runs a multi-service center in the building.

> *"I love the expression 'the understanding of the heart.' It seems to me that understanding is the keynote of true love, just as misunderstanding is fertile soil for hatred."*
> —Mother Mary Joseph Rogers

Denison House girls' basketball team, 1930

C12: Site of Denison House

93 Tyler Street

Denison House, a woman-run settlement house, occupied three buildings across the street from the Quincy School for fifty years. Founded in 1892 by the College Settlement House Association, Denison House was directed by **Helena Dudley** (1858-1932) and **Vida Scudder** (1861-1954), a Wellesley College professor. Their shop sold crafts produced by local women. They ran a medical dispensary, a milk station, and taught English. The heritage of Lebanese, Syrian, and Italian immigrant women was honored through crafts and folk dancing. Dudley believed women's greatest need was for a living wage and helped organize the Women's Trade Union League (see C16). When aviator **Amelia Earhart** (1897-1937) was a social worker there, she showered Boston with leaflets from a plane announcing a Denison House street fair.

Amelia Earhart

After an earlier association with Chicago's settlement house, Hull House, labor organizer **Mary Kenney O'Sullivan** (1864-1943) worked for a time at Denison House. She lived there with her husband, John F. O'Sullivan, labor editor of the *Boston Globe*, and their three children. After his sudden death in 1902, she managed a model tenement and continued her labor organizing activities. She was one of the principal founders of the National Women's Trade Union League at Faneuil Hall in 1903 (see D17). O'Sullivan supported many union activities, including the 1912 Lawrence textile strike. She was a strong supporter of woman suffrage and opposed the entry of the United States into World War I, joining the

Mary Kenney O'Sullivan

Women's International League for Peace and Freedom. In 1914, she became a factory inspector under the Massachusetts Department of Labor and Industries.

C13: Site of Rose Lok Home

Tyler Street (next to Denison House)

The first and possibly only Chinese American woman pilot to solo at what is now known as Boston's Logan Airport, **Rose Lok** (b. 1912) grew up on Tyler Street next to Denison House. She was only twenty when the U. S. Department of Commerce granted her a pilot's license in 1932. Although her parents resisted her desire to fly at first, they finally relented. She was the only woman in the group of twelve Chinese American Bostonians who formed the Chinese patriotic Flying Club to assist in the defense of China

Rose Lok

from Japan's invading forces. In 1996, she was memorialized with a tree at the International Forest of Friendship established by the Ninety-Nines, a long time association of women' pilots, in Atchison, Kansas, Amelia Earhart's hometown.

☞ *Directions: Continue to the end of Tyler Street noticing the mural of the Chinese New Year in Tai Tung Park at the corner. Turn right on Oak Street. Cross Harrison Street and turn right on Ash Street. Enter the Boston Chinatown Neighborhood Center.*

C14: Chinatown Community Mural: *Unity and Community*

Chinatown Neighborhood Center, 38 Ash Street

Formerly occupying the outside wall of a four-story building, a photographic reproduction of the mural *Unity and Community* has been installed in the main lobby of the Boston Chinatown Neighborhood Center. In this mural, Chinese-American women are honored for their many roles in Asian-American community life. Designed by **Wen-Ti Tsen** and **David Fichter** in 1986, the colorful painting shows a woman garment worker sewing a long piece of fabric which weaves through the composition and represents women's contribution to the

cohesiveness of the community. Before the liberalization of immigration laws, fewer than twenty percent of Chinatown's residents were women.

☞ *Directions: Return to Oak Street. As you cross Washington to Tremont Street, notice the friezes topping the new Quincy School designed by artist* **Maria Termini**, *using drawings by children in the old Quincy School. Cross Tremont Street and walk through the park passing the Church of All Nations. Continue on the walkway under the buildings to Warrenton Street.*

C15: Site of YWCA "Working Girls Home"

68 Warrenton Street

In 1873 the Boston YWCA built a six-story double house building on this site for "the good of working women." The location not only offered housing but training with the hope of finding "new and proper avenues of employment for

Unity and Community Mural

women" as well as "to protect them in their rights." Of the seventy women who lived in the building at the time of the Great Fire that year, thirty-four lost jobs and the YWCA established a sewing business to employ them. In 1908, the building had 212 boarders and had served a total of 2,645 women during the previous year. In 1895, the residents, hoping to escape the summer heat, raised money to create a roof garden on top of the building. They planted window boxes, added deck chairs, awnings and even cots. In anticipation of the opening of new headquarters at 140 Clarendon Street, the YWCA closed the building in 1927 (see BBW7).

☞ *Directions: Turn left on Stuart Street and cross it to the Transportation Building at 8-10 Park Plaza. On the corner, note the New England School of Law, the successor to the Portia Law School founded for women on Beacon Hill (see B4). Walk through the Atrium of the Transportation Building to Boylston Place.*

"We are just like soldiers patrolling in a just cause ...not one of us will flinch until we have won."
—Julia O'Connor [Parker]

Julia O'Connor [Parker]

C16: Boston Women's Trade Union League
5 Boylston Place
During the Great Depression, the Boston Women's Trade Union League maintained offices and a soup kitchen in this building owned and occupied on the upper floors

by Boston's exclusive Tavern Club for men. Soon after the National WTUL was established at Faneuil Hall in 1903, the Boston branch assisted women workers in forming trade unions and aiding strikes, including the telephone operators' strike of 1919 (see C4). Although upper middle class women reformers began the BWTUL, women workers joined and held major offices. Among the presidents were telephone operators **Julia O'Connor [Parker]** (see C4) and **Rose Finkelstein Norwood** (1891-1980). For fifty years they also helped organize Boston library workers, retail clerks, and office cleaners.

☞ *Directions: Continue through Boylston Place. Note the new site of some Emerson College buildings at 10 Boylston Place (see BBE7). Turn left to Park Square.*

C17: Park Square: Women Editors, Artists, and Entrepreneurs
Park Square at Boylston Street
The Park Square area and the block on Boylston Street across from the Public Garden was once a center for women editors, artists, social activists, and entrepreneurs who had offices in the

"Fiction is of great value to any people as a preserver of manners and customs... No one will do this for us; we must ourselves develop the men and women who will faithfully portray the inmost thoughts and feelings of the Negro with all the fire and romance which lie dormant in our history, and, as yet, unrecognized by writers of the Anglo-Saxon race."
—Pauline E. Hopkins, from her 1900 book *Contending Forces, A Romance Illustrative of Negro Life North and South*

small buildings that lined the street. Novelist **Pauline Hopkins** (1856-1930) edited *The Colored American* from 1900 to 1904 in an office at 5 Park Square. Her goal was to publish a journal devoted to "the development of Afro-American art and literature." She included a series of articles, *Famous Women of the Negro Race*, and reported the news of the rejection of **Josephine St. Pierre Ruffin's** New Era Club for membership in the General Federation of Women's Clubs in 1902 (see B17). Other publications edited by women with offices in Park Square include *Our Bodies Ourselves*, published by the Boston Women's Health Collective in 1970, and *Equal Times*, a newspaper for working women published in the mid-1970s and early 1980s. The Collective is located now in Somerville.

Many women artists studied and had studios in this area. Beginning in the 1890s until the mid twentieth century, women dressmakers, milliners, physicians, teachers, and artists working in many mediums had studios or offices on Boylston Street in the block across from the Public Garden. Conveniently placed among them by 1940 was the shop and lunchroom of the Women's Educational and Industrial Union.

The Crittenton Women's Union.

WEIU's first program was a shop selling women's crafts and food, but it rapidly moved into job training, placement, and protection of women workers. In recent years it instituted training for licensed home day care providers and created a transitional housing programs for single mothers. **Dr. Harriet Clisby** (1831-1931) founded the WEIU together with a group of prominent Boston women. **Mary Morton Kehew** (1859-1918) led the union from 1892 until her death. Under her direction, the union continued to offer vocational training but also lobbied for legislation to protect women workers. She supported her arguments with solid social science research. Kehew was active in the programs at Denison House (see C12) and worked to foster trade unions among women workers, becoming the first president of the National Women's Trade Union League organized in Boston in 1903 (see C16).

☞ *Directions: Cross Boylston Street and enter the Public Garden. For the location and descriptions of fountains designed by women sculptors, see BBE1.*

C18: Site of Women's Educational and Industrial Union
264 and 356 Boylston Street
The Women's Educational and Industrial Union, which has served Boston women continuously for nearly 130 years, was at two different sites on Boylston Street for sixty years. In 2004, WEIU renamed itself the Women's Union and moved downtown from this site to One Washington Mall. In 2006, they merged with Crittenton, a Boston-based housing and workforce development agency established in 1824. The new institution is called

An accounting class at WEIU, ca. 1940

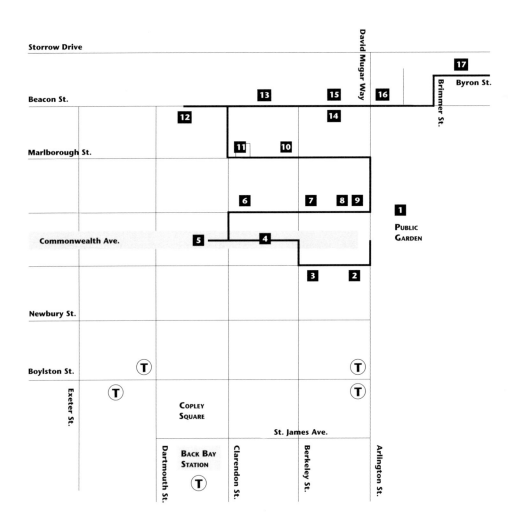

Storrow Drive

David Mugar Way

17

Brimmer St.

Byron St.

Beacon St.

13   **15**   **16**

12   **14**

Marlborough St.

11   **10**

6   **7**   **8 9**

1

PUBLIC GARDEN

Commonwealth Ave.   **5**   **4**

3   **2**

Newbury St.

Boylston St.   (T)   (T)

(T)   (T)

Exeter St.

COPLEY SQUARE

St. James Ave.

Dartmouth St.

BACK BAY STATION

(T)

Clarendon St.

Berkeley St.

Arlington St.

Back Bay Walk East

Use this map for all "BBE" sites

(T) = **MBTA stop**

(M) = **historic marker**

Back Bay Walk East

"Educators, Artists, and Reformers"

The Back Bay, originally a mudflat, was filled in with gravel brought from suburban Needham by train between 1852 and 1890. The land is flat, with streets laid out in a straight grid. The cross streets are conveniently named alphabetically from A to H. This elegant neighborhood includes Commonwealth Avenue with its tree-lined mall of grass, center walking path, and sculptures, as well as the "uptown" shopping area with high-end stores, art galleries, and restaurants.

The Back Bay East Walk starts and ends at the Public Garden. The sites highlight the work of women in the arts and in education, and women who led the way in environmental protection, suffrage, and peace.

Time: 1 1/2 hours
Begins: Boston Public Garden
☞ **Directions:** Enter the Public Garden at the corner of Beacon and Charles streets.

BBE1: The Public Garden and Fountains by Women Sculptors

Beacon, Charles and Arlington Streets
The Public Garden opened in 1837 as a private space, but grew into a public park with its lagoon, swan boats, seasonal plantings, fountains, and sculpture. The newest sculpture, *Make Way for Ducklings,* modeled on the ducklings in Robert McCloskey's book of the same name, is by local sculptor, **Nancy Schön**. Women also designed the sculptures for four fountains in the Public Garden. Using the map below, begin with the ducklings (V).

Map by Karen Tenney

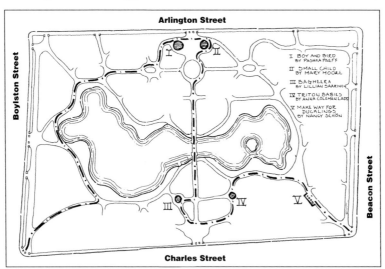

Follow the path to the left to *Triton Babies* (IV) by **Anna Coleman Ladd** (1878-1939), given by **Elizabeth Sturgis Grew Beal**. Continue to *Bagheera* (III) by **Lillian Swann Saarinen**. Named for the panther in Rudyard Kipling's *Jungle Book*, it was given to the garden by friends of the sculptor. Cross the bridge over the lagoon to the Arlington Street entrance. On your right is *Small Child* (II) by **Mary Moore** (1881-1967), the gift of **Margaret Tenney Tozzer**. On your left is *Boy and Bird* (I) by **Bashka Paeff** (1893-1979), a Russian immigrant who studied at the Museum School and gave the sculpture to the Public Garden.

Note: Thomas Ball's sculpture of Charles Sumner. Although **Anne Whitney's** model won the blind competition, the Boston Arts committee rejected it when they learned that the sculptor was a woman, choosing Ball's instead. Whitney later installed her version in Harvard Square in 1902 (see B15).

☞ *Directions: Exit at Arlington Street. Turn left. Turn right on Commonwealth Avenue.*

Amy Beach

woman to be performed by the New York Symphony Orchestra. Her standing as a composer led her to be commissioned to write the *Festival Jubilate* for chorus and orchestra which was played at the dedication of the Woman's Building during Chicago's 1892 World's Columbia Exposition. Beach's *Gaelic Symphony* was performed by orchestras throughout the country. In 1900, she premiered her own piano concerto with the Boston Symphony and later performed it in Europe. In addition to her larger pieces, Beach composed choral works, piano pieces, and over 150 popular songs.

BBE2: Home of Amy Beach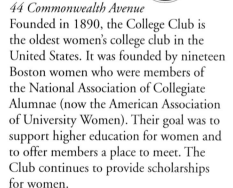

28 Commonwealth Avenue
Amy Beach (1867-1944) is one of America's most noted composers. Her work, which has been revived in recent years, is enjoying a new popularity. She began her career as a concert pianist, but after her marriage to Dr. Henry Harris Beach, she turned her talents to composition. When her *Mass in E flat major*, which took three years to complete, was performed by the Handel and Haydn Society with the Boston Symphony Orchestra in February 1892, it was the first work by a woman to be performed by the Society. In the same year her aria for an alto soloist was the first work by a

BBE3: College Club

44 Commonwealth Avenue
Founded in 1890, the College Club is the oldest women's college club in the United States. It was founded by nineteen Boston women who were members of the National Association of Collegiate Alumnae (now the American Association of University Women). Their goal was to support higher education for women and to offer members a place to meet. The Club continues to provide scholarships for women.

☞ *Directions: At Berkeley Street, cross to the Commonwealth Avenue Mall.*

From left to right: Jane, Barbara, Diane, Maureen, Evelyn, Ginny, Mary Jane, Julie, Danielle, Fran, and parents Julia and Dan O'Neil at Boston's Easter Parade in 1953

BBE4: Easter Parade, Julia Oliver O'Neil

Commonwealth Avenue Mall

Julia Oliver O'Neil (1909-78) and her ten daughters became famous in the Commonwealth Avenue Easter Parade. Every year, between 1940 and 1959, she made matching outfits for her daughters. Their picture was printed in journals and newspapers all over the world.

☞ *Directions: Walk down Commonwealth Avenue Mall. Cross Clarendon Street.*

BBE5: Statues by Theo Ruggles Kitson

Commonwealth Ave Mall, near Clarendon Street

Among the statues on the Commonwealth Avenue Mall created by women is the group honoring Mayor Patrick Collins created by **Theo Ruggles Kitson** (1871-1932) and her husband, Henry Hudson Kitson. The Collins statue is flanked by two women: one symbolic of Ireland, his birthplace, and the other of America. Kitson, who was known nationally for her Civil War memorials, including one of the nurse **Mother Bickerdyke** in Galesburg, Illinois, also created the statue of Thaddeus Kosciuszko in the Boston Public Garden. The Kitsons maintained a studio in Brookline.

☞ *Directions: Walk back to Clarendon Street. Turn left. Turn right on Commonwealth Avenue.*

BBE6: Site of Simmons College Graduate School of Social Work

51 Commonwealth Avenue

The Simmons College Graduate School of Social Work, founded in 1904, operated at this site for many years before moving to the college's main campus in The Fenway. It was the first school of social work to be affiliated with an institution of higher learning. When Simmons College was established as a women's college in 1899, Henry LeFavour, the first president, explained that the college hoped to prepare young women to earn their own livings. Recognizing that the college's goal was controversial, he explained: "Whether society ought to be constituted so that women should not need to earn their own living is a debatable question, but it is evident that the trend of society is now in the other direction." When the college opened, it offered training in household economics, secretarial studies, library science, and general science. The household economics course developed out of the Women's Educational and Industrial Union's School of Housekeeping (see C18). Social work was added next, followed by salesmanship and public health nursing. The salesmanship program—officially, the Prince School of Education for Store Service—also developed out of the Women's Educational and Industrial Union. Founded in 1905 by **Lucinda W. Prince** (1862-1935), the program became so popular that Prince soon teamed up with Simmons College to offer teacher training courses for her instructors. By 1915, the program was given its own name—the Prince School of Salesmanship—and it was administered jointly by Simmons and the Union.

On the right, the former Simmons College Graduate School of Social Work at 51 Commonwealth Avenue. To its left is 49 Commonwealth, the site of the Prince School of Salesmanship in the late 1940s.

By 1918, Simmons assumed complete responsibility for the school which was located at 49 Commonwealth Avenue (next to the School of Social Work) in the late 1940s. The Simmons College main campus is located on The Fenway. It offers an undergraduate liberal arts program and twelve graduate programs, including the only women's Master of Business Arts program. The MBA program is housed at 409 Commonwealth Avenue.

The School of Social Work building was owned by **Isabella Stewart Gardner's** father-in-law, John L. Gardner, who willed it to his son George, who gave it to Simmons. He was influenced by his mother, **Eliza Endicott Peabody Gardner**, whose life-long interest in social work convinced her son that this was the most appropriate use of their family home.

☞ *Directions: Continue down Commonwealth Avenue, passing No. 27. Formerly owned by the Massachusetts General Hospital and called Herrick House for its donor, Robert F. Herrick, the building was a residence for women who were student dieticians from 1942 to 1955.*

BBE7: Emerson College buildings
21 to 23 Commonwealth Avenue
Although Emerson College has moved to Boston's theater district, its first buildings were at this site. Emerson College was established as a school of public speaking in 1880. In the early years, most of its graduates became teachers. With the introduction of radio production to its curriculum, Emerson began to expand its offerings to a wide range of courses and experiences in communication. One of its most distinguished graduates was **Elma Lewis** (1922-2004), a committed community activist. She founded the Elma Lewis School of Fine Arts in Roxbury in 1950 in order to bring arts

Elma Lewis

"When I leave here, the body of my work will be all these wonderful people out there in the world, doing great things."
—Elma Lewis

to the African American community, especially to young people. She expanded her school to become the National Center of Afro-American Artists between 1969 and 1980. Her production of *Black Nativity* by Langston Hughes is still performed in Boston during the Christmas season. Emerson College awarded Elma Lewis an honorary Doctor of Humanities degree in 1968 (see BBW10).

BBE8: Boston Center for Adult Education

5 Commonwealth Avenue
Founded in 1933, the Boston Center for Adult Education was the first private, nonprofit adult education center in New England. It offers a range of courses in the humanities, arts, sciences, and professional development. One participant whose course at the Center led to a career in poetry was **Anne Gray Sexton** (1928-74). At the age of twenty-eight she took John Holmes's poetry workshop. She began writing poetry as mental therapy,

but soon became well known. Suffering from mental depression, she once said, "Poetry saved my life." She was awarded the Pulitzer Prize for her collection, *Live or Die*, in 1967. Although she committed suicide, many of her poems call out for life. She said, "I say Live, Live because of the sun,/ the dream, the excitable gift."

BBE9: Home of Sarah Choate Sears

One Commonwealth Avenue
Artist and art collector **Sarah Choate Sears** (1858-1935) and her husband Joshua Montgomery Sears lived in this Boston mansion in the first decades of the twentieth century. A graduate of the School of the Museum of Fine Arts, Sarah Sears painted portraits and still lifes and later took up photography. A supporter of local artists, Sears was the only woman incorporator of the Society of Arts and Crafts (see BBW18). She also was active in the work of the Copley Society (see BBW16). Sears was a patron of post impressionist painter Maurice Prendergast, and collected paintings by the early moderns and impressionists. Among them was her acquaintance, American-born **Mary Cassatt** (1845-1926), whose paintings are treasured by museums worldwide.

Regal Lillies, watercolor by Sarah Choate Sears

☞ *Directions: Turn left on Arlington Street. Turn left on Marlborough Street.*

BBE10: French Library and Cultural Center

43 Marlborough Street

Originally organized by members of French-American organizations working toward the liberation of France during World War II, the French Library and Cultural Center opened in 1945. Many women have been involved in creating and expanding the library. Led by **Belle P. Rand** (1869-1956), ten women and men, half French and half Americans, signed the articles of incorporation. Boston sculptor **Katharine Lane Weems** (1899-1989) donated her mansion to the Library in 1961. Under the leadership of **Edna Doriot**, an adjacent building was acquired in 1976. The goal of the center is to promote French language and culture. In addition to maintaining its library and archives, the French Library sponsors a film program, translation services, and cultural programs including a Bastille Day celebration with dancing on Marlborough Street.

☞ *Directions: Continue on Marlborough Street. Turn right on Clarendon Street.*

"Busy all day with my address for woman's suffrage meeting in the evening...Wendell Phillips made the concluding speech of the evening. He was less brilliant than usual, kept referring to what I had said. I thanked him for this afterwards, and he said that my speech had spoiled his own; that I had taken up the very points upon which he intended to dwell."—Diary of Julia Ward Howe, January 28, 1881

BBE11: Harriet Hemenway and the Massachusetts Audubon Society

273 Clarendon Street

Harriet Lawrence Hemenway (1858-1960) lived here when in 1896 she founded the Massachusetts Audubon Society with her cousin, **Minna Hall** (1851-1941). They were protesting the slaughter of birds for feathers to ornament women's hats. It was estimated that five million American birds of about fifty species were being killed annually for this purpose. Hemenway and Hall invited groups of women to tea and convinced about nine hundred of them to give up wearing feathered hats. Their next move was to invite some prominent men to join them to start the Audubon Society with a goal of protecting birds. Although national legislation took a little longer, by 1897 Massachusetts had passed a bill outlawing trade in wild bird feathers.

☞ *Directions: Continue on Clarendon to Beacon, turn left.*

BBE12: Home of Julia Ward Howe

241 Beacon Street

Julia Ward Howe (1819-1910) moved to an apartment at this site in 1879 a few years after the death of her husband, Samuel Gridley Howe. During this period she served as president of the Massachusetts and New England Suffrage Associations and worked on the national level to negotiate the reunion of the two branches of the suffrage association that split in 1860 over the 15th Amendment. Active in the women's club movement, she was a long time president of the New England Women's Club and helped found the Association for the Advancement of Women and the newer General Federation of Women's Clubs. In 1908 Howe was the first woman to be elected to the American Academy of Arts and Letters. By the time of her death, she was revered as a Boston institution. Hundreds of people were turned away at her memorial service in Symphony Hall where four thousand people joined in singing *The Battle Hymn of the Republic*, the hymn she wrote fifty years before (see also B2).

☞ *Directions: Walk back down Beacon to Clarendon Street. Cross Beacon Street.*

> *"...her people work as they feel she would have wanted them to do and the place must always remain live for that was the idea in the original conception [of Fenway Court] and in the execution of the idea, a living message of beauty in art to each generation."*
> —Olga Monks, Isabella Stewart Gardner's niece, in a letter written shortly after Gardner's death in 1924

Isabella Stewart Gardner

BBE13: Site of Home of Isabella Stewart Gardner

150-152 Beacon Street

While she lived at this address, **Isabella Stewart Gardner** (1840-1924) created one of Boston's most notable places, the Gardner Museum, a magnificent Renaissance Palace located in the Fenway. She called it Fenway Court. Opened in 1903, the museum houses a world-renowned permanent art collection. Her goal was to educate and provide pleasure for the public "forever." Gardner first displayed her paintings in this Beacon Street building which, like Fenway Court, was always filled with flowers and where she was the center of a salon of early twentieth century artists, musicians, and writers. Considered an eccentric by some and a genius by others, Gardner was known for her independent attitude and support of the talent in others on her own terms.

☞ *Directions: Continue down Beacon across Berkeley Street.*

BBE14: Gibson House Museum

137 Beacon Street

When **Catherine Hammond Gibson** (1804-88) had her home built on Beacon Street in 1860, she was a pioneer in the settlement of the Back Bay which was built on newly-filled land. Her husband, John Gardner Gibson, a sugar merchant, had been lost at sea and so Catherine moved to the house with her son, Charles Hammond Gibson. Charles Gibson's wife, **Rosamond Warren Gibson** (1846-1934), moved into the mansion in 1871. She had received the traditional education given to upper-class women in her day, learning French and taking dancing lessons from dancing master Lorenzo Papanti. When the Gibson House opened to the public in

Gibson House Museum

1957, **Marjorie Drake Ross** (1901-97), a specialist on the decorative arts and author of *The Book of Boston* series, helped to acquire appropriate objects for the Gibson House and directed the cataloging of the collection. Today, museum tours include interpretive stories of life both "upstairs" and "downstairs" in Victorian Boston. The Victorian Society's New England chapter has been based here since 1974. The society is an advocate for historic preservation, and offers walking tours and lectures on the Victorian era.

BBE15: Fisher College
102-118 Beacon Street
Fisher College was founded in 1903 by Myron C. and Edmund H. Fisher to provide business education for women in a two-year program. In 1939 it moved to this site, the former home of Henry and **Alice Spaulding King**. The building is noted for its elegant features including a marble hanging stairway.

The curriculum has been expanded to offer courses in communication, criminal justice, early childhood education, fashion merchandising, and hotel management. Students come from all over the United States and twelve different countries. Except for continuing education programs, the college was open only to women until 1998.

☞ *Directions: Continue on Beacon Street. Cross David Mugar Way.*

BBE16: The Winsor School, Schools for Girls
95-96 Beacon Street
Boston's tradition of establishing independent schools for girls is reflected in this site. The Winsor School, founded in 1886, was located in various Back Bay sites including this one until it moved to its present location on Pilgrim Road, near Boston's Fenway, in 1910. The school grew rapidly under the direction of **Mary Pickard Winsor** (1880-1950), who served as its headmistress from its founding until 1922. Many of the students in the first class went on to college, fulfilling the school's mission of college preparation for young women.

Several other independent schools for girls began in the Back Bay. The Haskell School for Girls was located on 314 Marlborough Street from 1903 to 1919. Conducted in the tradition of progressive education, the school was founded by **Mary Elizabeth Haskell** (1873-1964). Haskell was an activist in the Boston community of her day and in addition to running her school, nurtured the education of promising Boston immigrants, including poet Kahlil Gibran. Haskell became the head of The Cambridge School in 1919, which later became the Cambridge School at Weston. The Brimmer and May School, now located in Chestnut Hill, began in the Back Bay. It was made up of a combination of The May School, founded by **Mary May** at 339 Marlborough Street at the turn of the twentieth century, the Brimmer School, built in 1914 on Brimmer Street, and the Classical School for Girls.

☞ *Directions: Continue on Beacon Street. Turn left on Brimmer Street and right on Byron Street.*

BBE17: Women's International League for Peace and Freedom: Florence Hope Luscomb and Emily Greene Balch

6 Byron Street

Between World Wars I and II, 6 Byron Street was the office of the Massachusetts Women's International League for Peace and Freedom. **Florence Luscomb** (1887-1985) was executive secretary of the office from 1929-1933. An early graduate of MIT, Luscomb gave up her career in architecture to work full time for the women's movement. After suffrage was passed, she was the executive secretary for the newly formed Massachusetts League of Women Voters and narrowly missed being elected to the Boston City Council. She became involved in the labor

Florence Hope Luscomb

movement and ran for governor in 1952, continuing her antiwar and civil rights activities until her death. During the time the WILPF office was here, **Emily Greene Balch** (1867-1961), the second American woman to earn the Nobel Peace Prize, served as national president. Balch was a native of Boston and a former Wellesley College professor. From 1919 to 1922, as first international secretary-treasurer of WILPF in Geneva, Balch launched the new organization and set up its guidelines. In 1946, Balch followed **Jane Addams** (1860-1935) when she earned the Nobel Peace Prize in recognition of her efforts and the work of WILPF.

☞ *Directions: Continue on Byron Street. Turn right on River Street to Beacon Street. Turn left to the corner of Beacon and Charles streets where the walk started.*

Emily Greene Balch

"I see no possibilities of social progress apart from fundamental changes on both the economic and the political side...Peace is too small a word for this."
—Emily Greene Balch

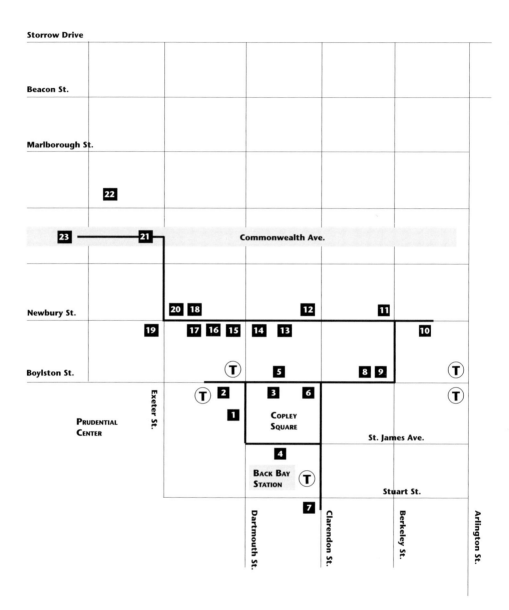

Back Bay Walk West

Use this map for all "BBW" sites

 = MBTA stop

 = historic marker

Back Bay Walk West

"Educators, Artists, and Reformers"

The Back Bay West Walk starts at Copley Square and ends at the Boston Women's Memorial. Focusing on women of the mid-nineteenth and early twentieth centuries, the sites demonstrate the high energy devoted by women to the arts and education, pointing out educational institutions, clubs, and art associations as well as women's sculptures.

Time: 1 1/2 hours
Begins: Boston Public Library, Copley Square
☞ **Directions:** Go into the library at the Boylston Street entrance.

BBW1: Boston Public Library

700 Boylston Street

The "BPL," as it is commonly known, has served as an intellectual and educational center for Boston women, from reformers to newly-arrived immigrants, since it opened in 1854. Housed in the elegant McKim building since 1895, the library was called a "noble treasure house of learning" by Russian immigrant, **Mary Antin** (1881-1949). She wrote, to be "in the midst of all the books that ever were written was a miracle as great as any on record" (see SE23). Many Boston women have also worked as library professionals including **Louise Imogen**

"Make the world better!"
—Lucy Stone to her daughter, Alice Stone Blackwell, upon Stone's death in 1893

✣

Lucy Stone by Anne Whitney

Guiney (1861-1920), who later became a respected poet and writer and filled a role as an ambassador between the Irish Catholic community and the Boston Brahmins.

Women pioneered children's services at the library. **Alice M. Jordan** (1870-1960) was the first Supervisor of Work with Children, serving from 1900 to 1940. In 1906, she founded the New England Round Table of Children's Librarians to provide a meeting ground for this emerging profession. Since 1960, the Round Table and the Massachusetts Library Association have sponsored the Jordan-Miller Storytelling Program in recognition of Jordan's commitment to storytelling. **Beryl Robinson** (1906-89), an African American, introduced storytelling to children in the BPL branches all over the city in the 1940s and 1950s. Her stories came from many cultures. In 1958-59, she produced and told stories on public television, extending her audience to children throughout eastern Massachusetts.

Several women are included in the library's art collection. The **Charlotte Cushman** Room on the third floor of the McKim building is named for one of Boston's favorite nineteenth-century dramatic actresses and art patrons, who was born in the North End (see N11). A bust by **Anne Whitney** (see B15) of **Lucy Stone** (see BBW23, D7), Boston suffragist and founder of the *Woman's Journal*, is displayed in Bates Hall, along with a bust of her daughter **Alice Stone Blackwell** (see BBW5) by **Frances L. Rich**.

Dioramas created by **Louise Stimson** (1890-1981) in the 1940s, also on the third floor of the McKim Building, depict miniature scenes of famous artists and their paintings (see N4).

BBW2: Women's Mural: Nine Notable Women of Boston

Boston Public Library,
Johnson Building entrance hall
Displayed in the entrance hall of the Johnson Building is the mural *Nine Notable Women of Boston*, originally created by **Ellen Lanyon** for the Workingmen's Co-operative Bank's centennial in 1980, in order to acknowledge the presence of women among its shareholders (see photo of mural on page 107). The mural was believed lost after the bank moved and changed ownership. After a search it was found at Simmons College which loaned it to the BPL so the mural could be displayed to the public. The notable women are: **Anne Hutchinson**, religious dissenter (see D1); **Phillis Wheatley**, first published African American poet (see BBW23, D21, C7); **Sister Ann Alexis** (1805-1875), hospital founder and administrator for the Daughters of Charity; **Lucy Stone**, suffrage leader and editor (see BBW23, D7); **Mary Baker Eddy**, founder of the Church of Christ, Scientist (see SE14 and D11); **Ellen S. Richards**, pioneer in ecology (see BBW8); **Mary Morton Kehew**, social reform leader (see C18); **Annie Sullivan**, teacher

of **Helen Keller** (see D20); and **Melnea Cass**, African American leader (see BBW7, SE16).

☞ *Directions: Walk into Copley Square.*

BBW3: Boston Marathon Finish Line, Tortoise and Hare Sculpture

Copley Square
In celebration of the 100th anniversary of the Boston Marathon in 1996, **Nancy Schön**, a former marathon runner, created the sculpture, *The Hare and the Tortoise*, at the finish line. Her *Make Way for Ducklings* statue is located in the Public Garden (see BBE1). A bronze circle recessed in the pavement displays the names of all the Boston marathon winners. Women were not allowed to enter the marathon as official runners until 1972 when **Nina Kuscsik** became the first female to be crowned with the laurel wreath. The first unofficial woman winner

Joan Benoit Samuelson winning in 1983

was **Roberta Gibb** in 1966. **Joan Benoit Samuelson**, who in 1984 was awarded the gold medal in the first women's Olympic marathon, won the Boston Marathon in 1979 and 1983. Other women Olympic gold medal winners who also placed first among women in the Boston Marathon were **Fatama Robba**, Boston winner in 1997 and 1998, and **Rosa Mota**, Boston winner in 1987, 1988, and 1990.

☞ *Directions: Look right across Copley Square.*

BBW4: Hotel and Restaurant Workers' Union

Fairmont Copley Plaza Hotel, Copley Square
Until the mid-1960s, only male waiters could work in local hotels organized by the Greater Boston Hotel and Restaurant Workers' Union. At that time, fifty-seven women waitresses, who were members of an all-women's union (Local 277) took their traveling cards to Local 24 of the union and asked for membership. When they were refused, the women sued. Supported by the Massachusetts Council Against Discrimination, the waitresses won their battle in June 1966. As members of the current local, Number 26, women now have the right to equal employment and equal pay in such union hotels as the Fairmont Copley Plaza, and are represented on the executive board of the union.

☞ *Directions: Look left across Boylston Street.*

BBW5: Massachusetts Woman Suffrage Association

Chauncey Hall, 585 Boylston Street
Chauncy Hall in 1913 was a "busy bee hive full of workers for women," according to the *Boston American* in 1913. It had housed the Massachusetts Woman Suffrage Association and the *Woman's Journal* since 1909 when they moved from 5 Park Street (see D7). In the last years of the suffrage campaign, the MWSA shared the building with the College Equal Suffrage Association, the Massachusetts Men's League for Woman Suffrage, the Boston Equal Suffrage Association for Good Government, and the New England Woman Suffrage Association. Women opponents to suffrage were not far. The Massachusetts Association Opposed to the Further Extension of Suffrage to Women had its office two blocks west, at the corner of Boylston and Exeter Streets. The group worked closely with the men's Massachusetts Anti-Suffragist Committee.

Alice Stone Blackwell (1857-1950), daughter of Lucy Stone and Henry Blackwell, edited the *Woman's Journal* for thirty-five years after her graduation from Boston University in 1881. She served as president of the MWSA from 1910 until women achieved suffrage in 1920. In addition to helping start the League of Women Voters, successor to the MWSA, Blackwell was active in many other causes including relief for Armenian refugees, the Women's Trade Union League, the National Association for the Advancement of Colored People, and the American

Boston Daily Globe,
August 19, 1920

Peace Society. As a young valedictorian, she had predicted her life of dissent, saying, "It's perhaps the first, but I don't mean it to be the last, old fence I shall break through."

☞ *Directions: Walk down Boylston Street to Clarendon Street. Turn right and enter the Trinity Church Parish House.*

BBW6: Sarah Wyman Whitman and Margaret Redmond Windows

Trinity Church and Parish House, Clarendon and Boylston Streets

Two women, **Sarah Wyman Whitman** (1842-1904) and **Margaret Redmond** (1867-1948), created stained glass windows in the Trinity Church Parish House. Redmond's work is also represented in Trinity Church itself. Whitman's window commemorates the life of the Reverend Phillips Brooks, first rector of the church. A devoted member of the church, Whitman taught Sunday Bible classes for women for thirty years. Upon the death of Brooks in 1893, Whitman and her class campaigned for three years before she was allowed to create the window. A stained glass window across from Whitman's window is dedicated to her memory. In addition to fabricating stained glass, Whitman painted landscapes, flowers, and portraits, and designed more than two hundred book covers for the Boston publisher Houghton Mifflin. In addition to creating the window, *Tree of Life*, in the Trinity Parish House to memorialize Boston painter **Susan Hinckley Bradley** (1851-1929), Margaret Redmond's windows inside Trinity Church include *Saul Anointeth David, David Plays before Saul*, and *Queen of Sheba before King Solomon* in the northwest vestibule. In the nave are her *Eight Apostles* and *The Evangelists*.

☞ *Directions: For the next site, either continue walking down Clarendon Street or look right to identify the site.*

BBW7: Young Women's Christian Association (YWCA)

140 Clarendon Street

The Boston Young Women's Christian Association, the first in the nation, was founded in 1866 by upper middle-class Protestant women. Led by **Pauline Durant** (1832-1917) until 1905, the YWCA hoped to guide and guard the young rural women coming to the city to work. The YWCA provided them with lodging and employment assistance. By the early twentieth century, the YWCA had added a School of Domestic Science and a popular gymnasium. The young women whom they served began to take an active role in the organization's management and established a busy club program. Confronting racism in the 1930s and 1940s, the YWCA integrated its branches and named **Lucy Miller Mitchell** (1899-2002) as the first board member of color in 1941. Mitchell, who became executive director of Associated Day Care Services of Metropolitan Boston, was a local and national pioneer in the development of standards for child care.

The YWCA on Clarendon Street, with its popular swimming pool and increased residential facilities, was constructed in 1929 (see C15). It is now named for **Melnea Cass** (1896-1978), a leader in increasing educational and occupational opportunities for African Americans. Known as "The First Lady of Roxbury," she was also a tireless activist for civil rights and a pioneer in the day care movement (see SE16). The YWCA supports training for non-traditional careers and runs a child care center. It also operates a transitional housing space and job training at Aswalos House in Dorchester. Most recently,

"If we cannot do great things, we can do small things in a great way."
—Melnea Cass

Melnea Cass

in 1998, it participated in opening the nation's first public housing facility for "grand families"—families consisting of grandparents raising their granchildren.

☞ *Directions: Return to Boylston Street and cross it on Clarendon. Turn right.*

BBW8: Rogers Building, Massachusetts Institute of Technology

501 Boylston Street
Although she was not directly connected with the Rogers Building, known as "Tech on Boylston Street" from 1886 to 1916, **Ellen Swallow Richards** (1842-1911) holds an important role in the history of the Massachusetts Institute of Technology. When she was admitted as a special student in chemistry in 1870, she became the first woman to study at MIT. She was awarded a B. S. degree three years later, but the doctorate for which she was qualified was refused her, it is believed, because the school did not want a woman to receive the first doctorate in chemistry. Richards, who pioneered the field of sanitary engineering and home economics, established a Woman's Laboratory at MIT in 1875 with funding from the Woman's Education Association. When her students were admitted to regular courses at MIT,

Richards closed the laboratory and, aided by **Ednah Dow Cheney** (1824-1904), **Lucretia Crocker** (1829-86), and **Abby W. May** (1829-88) (see D12), established a parlor and reading room for women students in a new MIT building. It was dedicated to the memory of Cheney's daughter **Margaret**, a student at MIT who would have been the second woman graduate had she not died of typhoid fever in 1882. In that year, four women received regular degrees. Richards continued to be connected with MIT as an instructor and laboratory scientist in sanitary chemistry and engineering, and in connection with her pioneering studies of air, water and food, is said to have coined the word "ecology."

Ellen Swallow Richards (left) testing the water at Jamaica Pond

☞ *Directions: Continue on Boylston Street. Turn left on Berkeley Street.*

BBW9: Museum of Natural History

234 Berkeley Street at Boylston (now Louis of Boston)
At its founding in 1830, women were not allowed to become members of the Boston Society of Natural History whose museum was at this site from 1864 to 1951, although they could use its resources. When the Society sought to

Interior of the Museum of Natural History, ca. 1900

Association sponsored summer classes for teachers at Annisquam (Gloucester), Massachusetts, in 1881. This led to the establishment of the Marine Biological Laboratory at Woods Hole on Cape Cod a few years later. In 1951 the museum, renamed the Museum of Science, moved to Science Park on the Charles River.

☞ *Directions: Walk to Newbury Street and turn right.*

BBW10: American Academy of Arts and Sciences
28 Newbury Street
Although the American Academy of Arts and Sciences has not occupied this building since 1955 and now is located in Cambridge, its roots are in Boston. Founded during the American Revolution to promote the arts and sciences, it was open only to men until 1943. The exception was astronomer **Maria Mitchell** (1818-89), who was elected to

Maria Mitchell

expand its membership in 1876, a great debate ensued. An opponent believed that "the presence of charming girls among the young students of science would be a great hindrance to any cold consideration of abstruse scientific thought." A proponent countered that women "would make as good members... and as interested an audience, as 9/10ths of the male members." Another supported the admission of women because they were "human beings even if they are of one sex."

Although fifteen women were soon admitted, women did not have a major influence until the Society established a Teachers' School of Science in 1870. When support for the school lagged, **Lucretia Crocker** (1829-86) (see SE8), supervisor of science for the Boston Public Schools, and philanthropist **Pauline Agassiz Shaw** (1841-1917) (see N13), raised the necessary funds to continue it. Noting the progress women teachers made in the school, the Woman's Education

"Until women throw off reverence for authority, they will not develop. When they do this...the truth which they get will be theirs and their minds will go on and on, unfettered." —Maria Mitchell

the academy in 1848 and for a century held that exclusive position in history. Soon after women were granted suffrage, the academy reconsidered its policy of electing only men to its membership. Even though a survey showed 147 members in favor and only 72 opposed, the academy did not elect women until 1943 when it admitted four women including another astronomer, **Cecilia Payne-Gaposchkin** (1900-79) of Harvard. In 1976 **Elma Lewis**, the founder of the National Center of Afro-American Artists in Roxbury, was elected to membership (see BBE7). Currently about twenty percent of the academy's new members each year are women.

Maria Mitchell was a favorite of nineteenth-century Boston women, and her annual visit to speak at the New England Women's Club was much celebrated. She grew up on Nantucket, where she learned celestial navigation from her father. In 1847 her discovery of a comet brought her fame and induction into the academy. Mitchell was a strong proponent of women's rights and helped found the Association for the Advancement of Women. She said, "The eye that directs a needle in the delicate meshes of embroidery will equally well bisect a star with the spider web of the micrometer." She also observed that, "Until women throw off reverence for authority, they will not develop. When they do this...the truth which they get will be theirs and their minds will go on and on, unfettered." Mitchell became Vassar College's first woman science professor and director of their observatory. Her observatory and birthplace are maintained by the Maria Mitchell Science Center on Nantucket Island.

☞ *Directions: Turn back on Newbury Street towards Berkeley Street.*

BBW11: Church of the Covenant, The Women's Lunch Place

67 Newbury Street

The Church of the Covenant has supported women since they were given the right to vote in all church matters in 1885. Member **Abbie Child** was the head of the Women's Board of Missions of the Congregational Church in the late nineteenth century. Member **Dr. Elsa Meder** was one of the first women ordained to the office of elder in the Presbyterian Church in New England. **Elizabeth Rice** and **Alice Hageman**, who were ordained in 1974 and 1975, were the first women to serve as pastors at a Back Bay church. When they were joined by **Donna Day Lower**, the church became the only one in the United States with three women clergy. The church sanctuary is noted for its Tiffany stained glass windows, including *Four Women of the Bible*, portraying **Miriam**, **Deborah**, **Mary of Bethany**, and **Dorcas**. Since 1982, when **Jane Alexander** and **Eileen Riley** opened the Women's Lunch Place, the church has served as a haven for poor women and their children.

BBW12: Junior League of Boston

117 Newbury Street

Boston's Junior League, established in 1907, is the second oldest Junior League in the country. Growing out of the nineteenth century sewing circle tradition, the league was first known as "The Sewing Circle League." Originally membership was by invitation only among the debutantes of the season. The league soon became interested in the social and industrial problems of the city and changed its name to the Junior League of Boston in 1916. The current Boston League has more than 1,500 members who contribute more than 30,000 hours

Geraldine Field, Ruth Talbot, and Ellen O'Donnell of the Junior League collecting books in 1935 for the annual campaign for the American Merchant Marine Library Association

BBW14: School of Fashion Design
136 Newbury Street
The School of Fashion Design was founded in 1934 by **Carolyn L. Dewing** and Donald Smith-Fedey as the Modern School of Applied Art. In 1936, Dorchester native **Isobel Sinesi** joined the faculty and was instrumental in adding fashion design to the curriculum. Serving as co-director from 1952 until her death in 1997, Sinesi led the school in developing its curriculum to focus entirely on fashion design.

"Freedom House...is an innovator, a catalyst, a launching pad ...to improve the way of life ...in cities."
—Muriel Snowden

Muriel Snowden

each year in community service programs. They welcome as members all women who are committed to volunteerism. The League focuses a significant part of its programming on the positive development of adolescent girls and works in collaboration with several organizations with similar goals.

BBW13: Gibbs College
126 Newbury Street
Gibbs College was formerly named the **Katharine Gibbs** School. Gibbs founded her first business school for women in Providence, Rhode Island, in 1911. She opened a Boston branch six years later. Originally designed to train young women in the new careers in office work that opened up to skilled women at the beginning of the twentieth century, the school is now coeducational and offers associate's degrees in office administration, computer networking, medical/clinical assisting, and graphic design.

BBW15: Muriel Snowden International High School
150 Newbury Street
In 1988, the Boston School Committee renamed Copley Square High School to honor long-time African American community activist **Muriel S. Snowden** (1916-88). With her husband, Otto, Muriel Snowden founded Freedom House, Inc., in Roxbury as a nonprofit community-based organization dedicated to human rights and advocacy for African Americans in Boston. Her leadership moved Freedom House into areas of urban renewal, minority employment, and educational equality for children as well as being a positive force for interracial cooperation in Boston. The high school encourages the study of international cultures and foreign languages, fields Snowden also fostered.

The building once housed the Boston Art Club, founded in 1855. Although women could not be members until the 1930s, they did exhibit there. Among the new members was **Meta Vaux Warrick Fuller** whose sculpture *Emancipation* stands in **Harriet Tubman** Square (see SE6).

BBW16: The Copley Society of Boston

158 Newbury Street
The oldest art association in America, the Copley Society was founded as the Boston Art Students Association in 1879 by the first graduating class from the Museum School of Boston's Museum of Fine Arts. The founders wanted a place to exhibit the work of young artists and to continue their Museum School associations. The organization changed its name to the Copley Society of Boston in 1901 and membership was no longer restricted to those persons with an affiliation. **Sarah Choate Sears** (see BBE9) and **Sarah Wyman Whitman** (see BBW6) served on the Copley Society's committees. Among other distinguished members were painter **Margaret Fitzhugh Brown** (1884-1972); **Lillian Westcott Hale** (1881-1963), known for her carefully drafted charcoal drawings; and **Marie Danforth Page** (1869-1940), whose portraits often depicted women and children. In addition to showing works by Boston women artists, the Society exhibited paintings by internationally known artists **Mary Cassatt** (see BBE9) and **Cecelia Beaux** (1855-1942).

"Every year we see these sisters of the brush and palette coming forward as doughty competitors to the men, and nowhere do they threaten more serious rivalry than in Boston." —William Howe Downes, 1896

BBW17: Guild of Boston Artists

162 Newbury Street
In addition to the art galleries along Newbury Street, many displaying the work of women artists and some owned or managed by women, is the Guild of Boston Artists. It is an association of painters, sculptors, and printmakers founded in 1914. Women have always been active in the guild and were among the charter members. One of its goals is to bring to public attention the work of young greater Boston artists. In addition to its public gallery, the guild sponsors art classes in its building.

Among women members was Bostonian **Lilla Cabot Perry** (1847-1933), whose paintings are included in the collections of the Museum of Fine Arts and the National Museum of Women in the Arts in Washington, D. C. She studied in Paris and was influenced by **Claude Monet**. She was his neighbor in Giverny for ten summers, beginning in 1889. Perry also taught and painted in Tokyo for three years. Other Boston women painters include **Adelaide Cole Chase** (1868-1944), who also studied in Paris and painted still life and portraits, especially of women and children; and painter **Gertrude Fiske** (1878-1961), who was a founder of the guild and was the first woman named to the Massachusetts Art Commission.

In 1930, Boston sculptor **Amelia Peabody** (1890-1984) held a major exhibition at the guild. Her sculpture *End of an Era*, depicting the last of the Boston one-horse cabs, was very popular and was acquired by the Museum of Fine Arts. Although she continued to create and exhibit her sculpture, Peabody was also a philanthropist. An ardent sportswoman and lover of animals, especially horses, she provided support to the new Tufts Veterinary School. She divided her time between her home at 120 Commonwealth

Avenue and her farm in Dover. Peabody continued creating sculpture late in life, turning to the medium of ceramics. She served on the boards of many Boston hospitals, donating funds—and sculptures—to them.

BBW18: Society of Arts and Crafts

175 Newbury Street

Women were active in the Society of Arts and Crafts from its beginning. It was founded in 1897 as an expression of the Arts and Crafts Movement and is the oldest nonprofit crafts organization in America. It encourages the creation and collection of the work of craft artists and awards an annual Medal of Excellence in Craft. Painter and art patron **Sarah Choate Sears** (see BBE9) was a member of the original incorporating committee and, along with **Sarah Wyman Whitman** (see BBW6), was an early officer. Women who were awarded the Medal of Excellence in the early years included: **Mary Crease Sears**, bookbinder; **Josephine H. Shaw** and **Margaret Rogers**, jewelers; **Sister Magdalen**, **Winifred Crawford**, and **Beatrix Holmes**, illuminators; **Lydia Bush-Brown**, batik dyer; and **Louise Chrimes**, needleworker.

☞ *Directions: Continue to Exeter Street.*

BBW19: Massachusetts Normal Art School Site

Northwest corner of Exeter and Newbury Streets

The Massachusetts Normal Art School, the predecessor of the Massachusetts College of Art, operated on this site from 1873 until 1886 when it moved to its present location at 621 Huntington Avenue. Because the school was a response to the Drawing Act of 1870 requiring free drawing classes for municipalities with a population of 10,000 or more, students training to be teachers had free tuition. In the first thirty years, eighty percent of the students were women.

☞ *Directions: Turn right on Exeter Street. On your left, note the Prince School, built as a Boston public coeducational grammar school in the 1870s.*

BBW20: Spiritualist Temple and Exeter Street Theater

Southeast corner of Exeter and Newbury streets

Though known as the Exeter Street Theater after 1913, this building was built as the First Spiritualist Temple in 1885. Young women played an important role in spiritualist meetings. They sometimes served on stage as mediums through whom it was believed a departed spirit was speaking. Two sisters, **Viola Berlin** and **Florence Berlin**, ran the Exeter Street Theater for many years, turning it into a popular place to see foreign films. The theater closed in 1984.

☞ *Directions: Walk down Exeter Street to the Commonwealth Avenue Mall. Turn left.*

BBW21: Women Sculptors on Commonwealth Avenue Mall

Commonwealth Avenue Mall

The statue of Samuel Eliot Morison near Exeter Street by **Penelope Jencks** is one of four statues created by women on the Commonwealth Avenue Mall before the installation of the Boston Women's Memorial. Jencks is well known as the sculptor of the **Eleanor Roosevelt** Memorial in New York's Riverside Park. Boston sculptor **Anne Whitney** (see B15) created the statue of Norwegian explorer

Leif Eriksson at the end of the mall near Charlesgate. **Yvette Compagnion** won the competition sponsored by the Argentine government to make the sculpture of Argentine president Domingo Sarmiento near Gloucester Street. **Theo Ruggles Kitson** worked with her husband, Henry Hudson Kitson, to create the group statue honoring Mayor Patrick Collins near Clarendon Street (see BBE5).

☞ *Directions: Look to your right at Commonwealth Avenue between Exeter and Fairfield.*

BBW22: Fanny Mason and Peabody Mason Music Foundation

211 Commonwealth Avenue
The Peabody Mason Foundation, established in the memory of **Fanny Mason** (1864-1948), a patron of musicians during her lifetime, gives grants to orchestras and performers and offers free concerts. The organization founded the Fanny D. Mason Professorship of Music at Harvard University. At her home on Commonwealth Avenue and in other venues, Fanny Mason sponsored public concerts by such well-known performers as Jan Paderwski, Pablo Casals, and Nadia Boulanger.

BBW23: The Boston Women's Memorial

Commonwealth Avenue at Fairfield Street
Installed in 2003, the Boston Women's Memorial represents three literary women: presidential advisor and correspondent **Abigail Adams** (see D15), suffragist and editor **Lucy Stone** (see D7), and the first African American published poet **Phillis Wheatley** (see C7 and D21). The bronze sculpture by New York artist **Meredith Bergmann** takes the women down off their pedestals so that they can use the pedestals for their work. The Memorial is the result of a twelve-year public process led by the Boston Women's Commission.

☞ *Directions: Follow the path beyond the Memorial to find words of famous women inscribed on plaques set in the ground next to the benches. To return to the Boston Public Library, walk back down the Commonwealth Avenue Mall to Exeter Street and turn right.*

"These women left a [written] legacy, which speaks to us, if we will listen. Women have always known that words were a tool, a tool that could give them access to a public voice."
—Meredith Bergmann

Boston Women's Memorial

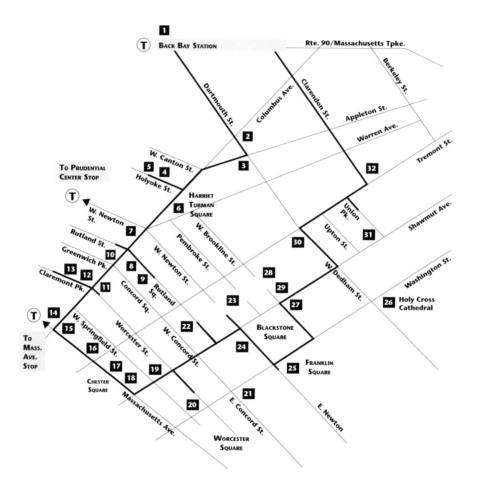

South End Walk

Use this map for all "SE" sites

(T) = MBTA stop

(M) = historic marker

South End Walk

"The Arts, Education, Medicine, and Reform"

The South End Walk starts at Back Bay Station, goes down Massachusetts Avenue, and then works it way back up and across to the Boston Center for the Arts. The walk presents a wide diversity of women, from mid-nineteenth through the twentieth centuries, particularly a flourishing African American community and their organizations. It takes us to two impressive sculptures, crafted by women, honors the area's immigrant populations including the newest group, the Latino community, and presents the work of women in settlement houses, hospitals, and schools.

A Victorian neighborhood, the South End was laid out in 1801 by architect Charles Bulfinch and built on filled land. It is a designated Landmark District featuring brick and brownstone row houses, cast iron fences and railings, and streets with center parks. The South End is home to an active arts community, as well as restaurants, cafés, and shops.

Time: 2 hours
Begins: Back Bay Station
☞ **Directions:** Enter Back Bay Station. Find the statue to A. Philip Randolph.

SE1: Back Bay Station and Neighborhood

Clarendon and Dartmouth Streets
In the Back Bay Station, **Tina Allen's** statue of A. Philip Randolph, founder of the Brotherhood of Sleeping Car Porters, signifies the importance of the role of porters in developing and sustaining African American communities all over the country, including one in the South End. Women in the union's Boston Ladies' Auxiliary served as hostesses at the nearby union headquarters every afternoon. Although one of the union's goals was for the men to make a living wage so their wives would not have to work, women did operate boarding houses where porters from other cities could stay between runs.

Los Angeles Sculptor Tina Allen, whose goal is to preserve the African American legacy, has sculpted many

Tina Allen's signature on her statue of A. Philip Randolph

other statues of African American leaders including one of **Sojourner Truth** in Battle Creek, Michigan.

☞ *Directions: Walk down Dartmouth Street crossing Columbus Avenue, noting the former Boarding house at 76 Dartmouth Street and, at 81 Dartmouth, the location of a funeral home operated by Millard F. Reid and his wife,* **Mattie Reid***, who took over the business when he died.*

SE2: Cora Reid McKerrow and the Reid Funeral Home

Cora Reid McKerrow

81 Dartmouth Street
Among the businesses serving the South End African American community was the Reid Funeral Home founded in 1926 by **Cora Reid McKerrrow** (1888-1984) and her brother Millard Fillmore Reid. After his death, McKerrow ran the funeral home for thirty years until she closed it in 1971. McKerrow was born into a family of fifteen children in Churchland, Virginia. When she first came to Boston, she worked as a chiropodist and beautician until she became a partner with her brother.

SE3: Rice School and Boston Normal School (former)

Corner of Dartmouth and Appleton Streets
The Boston Normal School, designed to train women teachers for the Boston Public Schools, became a separate entity when it moved from Girls' High to the top floors of the Rice School in 1876 (see SE23). Founded in 1852, the two-year normal course trained women to be assistants to male masters in primary and grammar schools. When the Normal School moved to the Rice School, women were required to be high school graduates and the course was one year, becoming two years in 1892. Women assistants taught in the two training schools: a boys' grammar school in the Rice School and a mixed primary school, the Appleton Street School (later the Bancroft School). By the time Boston Normal was renamed Boston Teachers College in 1922, it had its own building on Huntington Avenue and, in 1925, a four-year program. In 1952 the Teachers College became part of the state college system and, as Boston State College, merged with the University of Massachusetts at Boston in 1965.

☞ *Directions: Turn right onto Appleton Street. Walk to Columbus Avenue, cross, and turn left. Turn right on Holyoke Street.*

SE4: Home of Susie King Taylor

23 Holyoke Street
The remarkable life of **Susie King Taylor** (1848–1912) is honored by a marker at this site. Born a slave, she was freed with her family when they escaped to the Union Army during the Civil War. She served as a teacher and a nurse with the army while still in her teens. After the war, she opened a school for African American children in Savannah, Georgia. After the death of her husband, she came north as a cook and settled in Boston before remarrying. In 1886, she helped organize Corps 67 of the Women's Relief Corps, an auxiliary to the GAR that served veterans, and became its president in 1893. In her book *A Black Woman's Civil War Memoirs, Reminiscences of My Life in Camp* published in 1902 in Boston, she protested the current treatment of African Americans in the United States.

Harriet Tubman in *Step on Board* (see photo of full statue on inside back cover)

SE5: Harriet Tubman House Site

25 Holyoke Street
The Harriet Tubman Crusaders, an African American branch of the Women's Christian Temperance Union in Boston, created the first Harriet Tubman House in 1904 as a residence for African American women who were excluded from the city's college dormitories and respectable rooming houses. The Crusaders rented a brownstone on Holyoke Street until 1909 when member **Julia O. Henson** donated her own townhouse at 25 Holyoke Street as a permanent headquarters for the organization's expanding programs. Harriet Tubman visited Boston several times in the late nineteenth and early twentieth centuries, often staying with Julia Henson at this site. In 1959, the Harriet Tubman House merged with other settlement houses in the area to form the United South End Settlements (USES) and erect a modern building at the corner of Columbus and Massachusetts Avenues (see SE15).

☞ *Directions: Return to Columbus Avenue. Cross and walk to Harriet Tubman Square at Pembroke and West Newton Streets.*

SE6: Harriet Tubman Square Statues: *Emancipation* by Meta Vaux Warrick Fuller and *Step on Board* by Fern Cunningham

Dedicated at a community-wide celebration on June 20, 1999, these two powerful statues by African American women sculptors stand as a testament to the African American drive for freedom. Although **Meta Vaux Warrick Fuller** (1877-1968) completed *Emancipation* in 1913 on the fiftieth anniversary of the Emancipation Proclamation, it was not cast in bronze until it was selected to be

Meta Fuller's statue *Emancipation* depicted a freedman and freedwoman as active agents moving out of slavery into the world

placed at Harriet Tubman Square. Instead of showing the paternalism of a white president freeing enslaved people, Fuller presented the freedman and freedwoman as active agents moving out of slavery into the world. Fuller was a community activist herself in addition to being a sculptor. She married Solomon Carter Fuller, America's first African American psychiatrist in 1909 (see SE21).

In *Step on Board*, Boston-based **Fern Cunningham** shows both the power and compassion of **Harriet Tubman** (1822-1913), the most famous "conductor" on the Underground Railroad. Among Cunningham's other public sculptures in Boston are *Earth Challengers* at the Joseph Lee School in Dorchester and *Sentinel* in the Forest Hills Cemetery.

☞ *Directions: Cross Columbus Avenue to the corner of West Newton Street.*

SE7: Union United Methodist Church
485 Columbus Avenue

The congregation of the church has been housed in this building since May 9, 1949, when **Mary McLeod Bethune** (1875–1955) gave the dedication speech to an overflowing audience. The church, which has had four locations, originated as an African American church in 1818 on the north side of Beacon Hill. When the church was located in Lower Roxbury in 1916, the Women's Home Missionary Society, under the leadership of **Hattie B. Cooper** (1862–1949), provided services for the growing population of African Americans in that area. The church continued these services in Lower Roxbury and now houses them in the Hattie B. Cooper Community Center which opened in 1975.

☞ *Directions: Continue down Columbus Avenue. Turn left at Rutland Square.*

"Why are female and minority students not taking courses in mathematics and science?"
—Lucretia Crocker

Lucretia Crocker

SE8: Home of Lucretia Crocker
40 Rutland Square

As the first woman supervisor in the Boston Public Schools, appointed in 1876, **Lucretia Crocker** (1829–86) pioneered the discovery method of teaching mathematics and the natural sciences during her decade-long tenure. Earlier, she joined **Abby May** (1829–86) and three other women in their successful drive to be the first women elected to the Boston School Committee (see D12). Previously, Crocker's ten years of service to the Teachers' Committee of the Freedmen's Aid Society included visits to schools in the South as well as selecting and training teachers and providing curriculum. She also taught at Antioch College under Horace Mann's presidency to illustrate her belief in women's right to higher education.

 Louise Chandler Moulton

SE9: Home of Louise Chandler Moulton
28 Rutland Square

An author, critic, correspondent, and hostess to literary notables of her day, **Louise Chandler Moulton** (1835–1908) was perhaps best known as a person who encouraged new talent and introduced American readers to new poets and writers. Her influence extended over both Boston and London where annually for six months in each place she held weekly salons for writers over a period of three decades. Among the people with South End roots who attended her salon was the Irish American writer **Louise Imogen Guiney** (1861–1920) (see BBW1). Chandler's own writings included poems, travel and narrative sketches, children's stories, and reviews frequently published in the journals and newspapers of her era. Like many other women of the time, Moulton was also interested in the practice of spiritualism.

☞ *Directions: Return to Columbus Avenue. Turn left. Turn right at Greenwich Park.*

SE10: Home of Estella Crosby
11 Greenwich Park
Estella Crosby (1890–1978), beautician and community activist, formed the Boston unit of the Housewives League with **Geneva Arrington** and **E. Alice Taylor**. The organization was active from the 1930s to the 1960s with units in many major cities. Its goal was to overcome economic and educational barriers to African American advancement. Crosby also operated a dry goods store with her husband and was active in trade unions.

☞ *Directions: Return to Columbus Avenue and turn right.*

SE11: Mildred Davenport's Silver Box Studio
522 Columbus Avenue
Mildred Davenport (1900–90) housed her dance studio at this address. Born in Roxbury, Davenport became a trailblazing dancer and renowned dance instructor. A graduate of Boston University's Sargent College, she taught physical education at Tuskegee Institute (later University) in Alabama from 1921 to 1932. Later she entered show business. In 1938 she danced her interpretation of African American spirituals with the Boston Pops. She appeared on Broadway with such

Mildred Davenport

revues as *Blackbirds* and *Flying Colors* and danced with white performers including Imogene Coca and Clifton Webb, virtually unprecedented for an African American dancer in that period. For more than five years she toured in the *Chocolate Revue* in New York, Baltimore, and Washington, D. C. When she put her dancing career behind her, she served as an officer in the Women's Army Corps during World War II. From 1947 to 1968, she worked for the Massachusetts Commission against Discrimination. She also founded the 464 Community Workshop, a fund raising auxiliary of the Women's Service Club which still presents an annual review called *464 Follies* (see SE16).

☞ *Directions: Continue down Columbus Avenue. Turn right at Claremont.*

SE12: Anna Bobbitt Gardner Academy of Musical Arts
1-3 Claremont Park
In 1932, **Anna Bobbitt Gardner** (1901-97) became the first African American women to be awarded a bachelor's degree from the New England Conservatory of Music. She operated at least five studios in Boston under the same name for more than sixty years. She first opened the Academy in 1924 in the basement of her home. She managed *Colored*

American Nights, featuring African American musicians at Symphony Hall, and produced local radio and television programs for an African American audience. In 1945, Gov. Maurice J. Tobin appointed her state director of Negro History Week programs to accompany fine arts exhibits at selected historic buildings. Succeeding governors reappointed her to the position. Since 1997, the New England Conservatory has granted a musician the Anna Bobbitt Gardner Lifetime Achievement Award.

Gladys A. Moore Perdue

SE13: Home of Gladys A. Moore Perdue

22 Claremont Park
Before the New England Conservatory of Music awarded degrees, **Gladys A. Moore Perdue** (1898–1998) was the first African American woman to receive a diploma from the institution when she received a Diploma in Pianoforte in 1924. From 1925 to 1931, she taught music at Tuskegee Institute. After she returned to Boston, the Albanian Church in South Boston appointed her as its organist for thirty years. Among her many performances in the South End was music accompanist for the *464 Follies* performed by the Women's Service Club (see SE11, SE16). For her one hundredth birthday,

the Back Bay Stompers, a jazz sextet comprised of New England Conservatory students, entertained Gladys Perdue and other residents of Goddard House in Jamaica Plain.

☞ *Directions: Return to Columbus Avenue and turn right. At 549 note the Lucy Parsons Radical Bookstore, named for anarchist* **Lucy Parsons** *(ca. 1853–1942), an African American labor organizer, who lived in Chicago.*

SE14: Mary Baker Eddy, Massachusetts Metaphysical College

571 Columbus Avenue
For seven years between 1882 and 1889, **Mary Baker Eddy** (1821-1910), founder of the Church of Christ Scientist (Christian Science Church), operated the Massachusetts Metaphysical College at this site. More than 4,000 students attended her classes during this period. Eddy also conducted church services in the building. A few years before moving here, the Christian Science Association had voted to organize as a church and ordained her as its pastor. Despite the death of her husband in 1882, she continued to move ahead. Here she published the first issue of the *Journal of Christian Science* and her sixth edition of *Science and Health*, which she would continue to revise throughout her life. The religion she founded grew rapidly and in 1895, the "Mother Church" was installed in its first building on Huntington Avenue. The domed building followed in 1906 (see D11).

☞ *Directions: Cross Columbus Avenue.*

> *"Truth is immortal. Error is mortal."*
> —Mary Baker Eddy

Harriet Tubman, the famous "conductor" of the Underground Railroad; the first Harriet Tubman House, which was named for her, opened in 1904

> *"I had reasoned this out in my mind, there was one of two things I had a right to, liberty or death; if I could not have one, I would have the other."*
> —Harriet Tubman

SE15: Harriet Tubman House

566 Columbus Avenue

The modern Harriet Tubman House is headquarters for the United South End Settlements (USES) which was a merger in 1959 of four independent agencies: the South End House branches, the Children's Art Centre, Lincoln House, and Hale House. The latter two were torn down during urban renewal (see SE22, SE31). The United South End Settlements built the present Harriet Tubman House in 1959 on the former site of the Hi-Hat, one of Boston's notable jazz clubs (see SE5). Serving the South End and Lower Roxbury, the mission of the USES is to act as a catalyst "to bring together the resources of individuals, the community, and the agency to promote the well-being of those at risk within the community, and to nurture personal and communal growth and development." Founded in 1885, the Ellis Memorial Center presently at 95 Berkeley Street is considered to be Boston's first settlement house.

Directions: Turn left on Massachusetts Avenue.

SE16: The Women's Service Club of Boston

464 Massachusetts Avenue

The Women's Service Club began as one of Mrs. Wilson's knitting clubs, organized by **Mary Evans Wilson** (1866–1928), when, during World War 1, members met to knit scarves and gloves for soldiers. Wilson and her husband, Attorney Butler Wilson, were organizers of the Boston branch of the NAACP, which had the largest membership in the national organization during its first decade, 1909–20. Mary Evans Wilson traveled throughout the northeast recruiting members for the NAACP. In Boston her knitting clubs produced 300 new women members. In 1919, the club, by then called the Women's Service Club, purchased this building and incorporated with a goal of providing service programs for the African American community. Among the club's former presidents was **Harriet Hall** (1890–1975), who co-founded the interracial Women's Republican Club on Beacon Hill in 1920. As president of WSC, she spearheaded the WSC's drive to allow African Americans to live in dormitories of local educational institutions. **Melnea Cass** (1896–1978) served as president for more than fifteen years. Cass initiated the Homemakers Training Program which certified domestic workers so they would be assured social security and other benefits. She worked to open employment for African Americans in stores and hospitals, helped found Freedom House, was president of the Boston NAACP, and a charter member of the anti-poverty agency ABCD. Known as the "First Lady of Roxbury," Melnea Cass is honored by having the Boston YWCA on

Clarendon Street named for her
(see BBW7).

*Directions: Continue down Massachu-
setts Avenue and cross Tremont Street.*

SE17: Chester Square: Anna Quincy Waterston, Harriet Boyd Hawes, the South End Historical Society, and Betty Gibson

532 and 530 Massachusetts Avenue
Before the widening of Massachusetts
Avenue in the 1950s, Chester Square was
an elegant park surrounded by a wrought
iron fence and centered with a fountain.
Among the notable women living there
with their families was writer **Anna Cabot
Lowell Quincy Waterston** (1812–99),
whose witty 1833 diary has recently
been republished. She was a minister's
wife and the daughter of Boston Mayor
Josiah Quincy. Archeologist **Harriet Boyd
Hawes** (1871–1945) was born and spent
her childhood on Chester Square. After
training at Smith College and joining
excavations in Crete, she became the
first woman to lead an archaeological
expedition when she discovered the
ancient town of Gournia on Crete. In
later years she also served as a volunteer
nurse during the Greco-Turkish War and
World War I.

The South End Historical Society
has worked to preserve the history and
restore the buildings of the South End.
The Society purchased 532 Massachusetts
Avenue in the 1970s and occupies the
parlor on the second floor which still has
many original features. Architect Luther
Briggs Jr. designed the building in 1860
for Francis and **Zervia Dane**. Realtor
Betty Gibson also helped revitalize the
South End. In the 1960s she moved to
530 Massachusetts Avenue to demonstrate
her commitment to the area's renewal.

*Directions: Continue along
Massachusetts Avenue.*

*"I dare
not fail."*
—Maria
Louise
Baldwin

Maria Louise Baldwin

SE18: The League of Women for Community Service

558 Massachusetts Avenue
The League of Women for Community
Service is one of the oldest African
American women's organizations in the
city. The League honored its first president
Maria Louise Baldwin (1856–1922) by
dedicating their library to her in 1921.
Baldwin was the first African American
woman headmaster in New England,
serving for over thirty years as head of the
Agassiz School in Cambridge. In 2002 in
her honor, the city renamed the school the
Baldwin School. Among other presidents
were **Josephine St. Pierre Ruffin**
(1842–1924), founder of the Women's
Era Club and publisher of the *Women's
Era* newspaper, and her daughter **Florida
Ruffin Ridley** (1861–1943), the second
African American teacher in the Boston
Public Schools (see B17). Other presidents
included **Wilhelmina Crosson** (1900–91),
another pioneering African American
teacher in the Boston schools who became
the second president of Palmer Memorial
Institute in Sedalia, North Carolina, a
preparatory school for African American
young people, and **Gladys Holmes**
(1892–1969), a Radcliffe graduate who

was an author, educator, and social worker. **Coretta Scott King** (1927-2006) lived here when she was a student at the New England Conservatory of Music. The building is believed to have been a station on the Underground Railroad when it was owned by James Farwell, a sea captain and anti-slavery activist.

☞ *Directions: Turn left on Shawmut Avenue and left on West Springfield Street where there is a community garden, operated by the South End-Lower Roxbury Land Trust.*

SE19: Louisa May Alcott School and Alcott residences

West Springfield Street and Shawmut Avenue
The presence of author **Louisa May Alcott** (1832-88) in the South End covers many areas and activities. The Louisa May Alcott School was on this site from 1910 until it closed in 1961. A settlement house named the Louisa May Alcott Club, located on 15 Oswego Street north of East Berkeley Street, offered activities to Italian and Jewish immigrants.

In addition, Louisa May Alcott herself lived off and on in the South End, both with her family and as an independent woman. As early as 1835, they lived in three locations in the South End, including rooms on Harrison Avenue and Beach Street, before moving to Concord in 1840. By 1848 the family was back, living in a small house on Dedham Street. For a brief time, Louisa assisted her sister **Anna B. Alcott** (1831-93) who operated a school on Canton Street. In later life, Louisa often spent summers with the family in Concord and winters in Boston; for example, in the winter of 1873 she brought her family to 26 East Brookline Street overlooking Franklin Square. The South End and Concord came together when Louisa rented a quiet room on

West Brookline Street for several months in 1868 where she wrote the sequel to *Little Women* (see B6).

☞ *Directions: Return to Shawmut, turn left. Turn right on Worcester Street.*

SE20: Bethany Home for Young Women

14-16 Worcester Street
Operated as a home for single young women by the Universalist Church at this site from 1890 to 1940, the Bethany Home was open to women of all faiths who paid a small entrance fee. The home was partly supported by Bethany Sisters Circles in churches throughout the state and beyond. It moved to 256 Newbury Street in the Back Bay where it still provides affordable housing for young women and is now known as Bethany Union.

☞ *Directions: Return to Shawmut and turn right. Stop at West Concord Street.*

Bethany Union, ca. 1920

SE21: View of New England Female Medical College, now the Boston University School of Medicine and the Dr. Solomon Carter Fuller Center

East Concord Street and East Newton Street at Harrison Avenue

Dr. Samuel Gregory founded the New England Female Medical College in 1848 because he believed having male doctors deliver babies offended female decency. Despite his limited goals, the college did open its doors to women for medical training and did employ a female faculty. Among the college's graduates in 1864 was **Dr. Rebecca Lee Crumpler** (1831–95) (see B9) who is considered to be the first professional African American woman doctor. **Julia Ward Howe**, **Ednah Dow Cheney**, and **Abby May** were among others who served on the Board of Lady Managers. In 1859 **Dr. Marie Zakrzewska** asked that a clinical department be added so students could get practical experience. When the college closed the clinic after she left in 1862, Zakrzewska and the clinic's board members founded the New England Hospital for Women and Children (see B11).

The New England Female Medical College moved to several different locations in the South End until 1870 when it erected its own building on East Concord Street. In 1873, Boston University (B. U.) took over the Female Medical College as its own School of Medicine, practicing homeopathy and making it coeducational. Women faculty from the Female Medical College who continued at the B. U. School of Medicine included **Dr. Adeline B. Church** (1846–1927) and **Dr. Mary Safford-Blake** (1834–91), who both taught gynecology, and **Dr. Caroline Hastings** (1841–1922), who taught anatomy. Safford-Blake is considered the first woman gynecologist. She was also involved in homeopathy,

"I have never worked so hard in all my life and I would rather do that than anything else in the world."
—Civil War Nurse

 Dr. Mary Safford-Blake

and made such a reputation as a Civil War nurse that she was called the "Cairo Angel." She later held a term on the Boston School Committee as did Hastings who served for six years.

The impetus for the Fuller Mental Health Center was the Fort Hill Mental Health Association organized in the mid-1960s by the Boston Alumnae Chapter of Delta Sigma Theta, an African American sorority. Volunteers from church and community organizations ran the association and advocated for mental health services for minority populations in Boston. In 1974 the center opened as part of the B. U. Medical Center. It was later named for Dr. Solomon Carter Fuller, America's first African American psychiatrist. His wife was **Meta Vaux Warwick Fuller**, the sculptor of *Emancipation* in Harriet Tubman Square (see SE6).

☞ *Directions: Continue on Shawmut and turn left on Rutland Street.*

SE22: South End House and Children's Art Centre

36-48 Rutland Street

Boston's settlement house movement was one of the earliest in the country. Patterned after Toynbee Hall in London's East End where university graduates lived or "settled" within the disadvantaged communities they hoped to serve, the movement in America was a response to the consequences of immigration, industrialization, and urbanization. Initiated in Boston by Robert A. Woods as Head Resident in 1891, the South End House had many locations in the South End and Lower Roxbury and included women's and men's residences (see SE31). College women in Boston also founded their own settlement house, Denison House (see C12). The present South End House is the home to the youth programs of the United South End Settlements. Its newly renovated building was built in 1840 by the Children's Friend Society as a home for orphaned children. Among its recent social workers was **Gladys Gusson** (1935–88) who counseled families, was a tenant advocate, and ran after-school groups and girls' clubs.

Long-time activist and Dominican community leader **Frieda Garcia** was president of USES from 1981 to 2001. A portrait of her hangs inside this building. She was the first director of La Alianza Hispana, a community based nonprofit organization providing a wide range of services to Latino families, founded by **Ana Maria Rodriquez**, a Boston teacher.

The Children's Art Centre offers a wide range of art and music for children under the sponsorship of the USES. **Annie Endicott Nourse** (1878–1965), a piano teacher, founded the South End Music School here in 1910. It merged with the Boston Music School Settlement in 1968 to become the Community Music Center of Boston at the Boston Center for the Arts (see SE32).

☞ *Directions: Return to Shawmut Ave. Turn left. Turn left on West Newton Street.*

Girls' High building, West Newton Street

SE23: Girls' High and Girls' Latin School Site

Between West Newton and Pembroke Streets, now the Thomas F. O'Day Playground
A high school for girls opened in 1852 after more than twenty-five years of efforts to provide high school education for girls. The new Girls' High opened on this site in 1870. Girls' Latin School was added as a separate school in the same building in 1877 (but with the same headmaster) after the first women elected to the Boston School Committee used their new political power to guarantee girls a Latin School education. The building was considered to be elegant with 66 classrooms "all well lighted and cheerful" and an assembly hall on the upper story. Girls' High continued at this site until 1954, but by 1907 all Girls' Latin School classes had moved into the new Boston Normal School building on Huntington Avenue (see SE3).

Girls continued to go to a Latin school separate from boys until 1972 when the Latin schools became coeducational, ending 337 years of a separate Latin school education for boys.

Mary Antin

"As time went by, I became an avid collector of materials to use in educational and informational programs…It is a wonderful way to show that we Arab-Americans have inherited a warm and beautiful culture, and that the Arabs have made many worthwhile contributions to Western civilization in the applied arts as well as the fine arts, the sciences, and literature."

—Evelyn Abdalah Menconi

Labeebee Hanna Saquet in costume for the Arabian Nights

"My schoolmates helped. Aristocrats though they were, they did not hold themselves aloof from me. Some of the girls who came to school in carriages were especially cordial. They rated me by my scholarship, and not by my father's occupation….It was a generous appreciation of what it meant for a girl from the slums to be in the Latin School, on the way to college."

—Mary Antin

SE24: Lebanese-Syrian Ladies' Aid Society

44 West Newton Street

When the Arab American community moved from South Cove to the South End, the women also moved the headquarters of the Lebanese-Syrian Ladies' Aid Society to 44 West Newton Street (see C9). Although the society continued its mission of providing aid and scholarships to the Arab American community, its mix of ages created an extended family. According to its historian, **Evelyn Shakir,** it served as a "benevolent matriarchy" for the young women who worked in the shops or attended nearby Girls' High School.

Among the graduates of Girls' Latin when it was at this site was **Mary Antin** (1881–1949). Born in Russia, Antin immigrated with her family to America in 1894. They eventually moved to the South End where Antin took advantage of the public schools and library. Her book, *The Promised Land*, was a best seller when it was published in 1912. A classic about the American immigrant experience, the book captures the heart of the South End of her youth, particularly in the New York streets area between what is now East Berkeley and the Massachusetts Turnpike, a community wiped out by urban renewal in the 1960s.

☞ *Directions: Walk back down West Newton Street and cross Shawmut Avenue.*

The cast from the 1930 Tercentenary production of *Arabian Nights* at Symphony Hall, Boston

Among the Arab American women who were the first to teach in the Boston Public Schools were art teacher **Labeebee Hanna Saquet** (1904–97) and media specialist **Evelyn Abdalah Menconi** (1919–2003). Both woman served as bridges between Arab Americans and the general public, beginning in 1930 when Saquet directed *Arabian Nights*, a Boston Syrian Tercentenary celebration presented at Symphony Hall. Menconi worked with Shakir on the *Arabic Hour* television program and was the curator of the William A. Abdalah Memorial Library at St. George Orthodox Church in West Roxbury, which offers a Memorial Cultural Series in her name. She wrote *Eastern Mediterranean Cooking*, and was co-editor of an issue of *Cobblestone* on Arab Americans.

☞ *Directions: Continue down West Newton Street to Washington Street at Franklin Square. Note the photographic display of working women on the kiosk at the Silver Line T stop on the corner.*

A bed chamber in the Franklin Square House

SE25: Franklin Square House

11 East Newton Street
A former well-known residence for working women and students, the Franklin Square House provided decent and safe housing for Boston women for more than forty years in the mid twentieth

century. In addition to individual rooms, the building had a ballroom on the first floor edged with curtained cubicles with couches, where the women could entertain their guests. A cafeteria provided breakfast, dinner, and box lunches. The Blue Goose restaurant on the main floor was open to the public.

Constructed as the St. James Hotel in 1868, the largest in Boston and able to accommodate 500 guests, the building became the New England Conservatory of Music in 1882. In 1902 the Rev. George L. Perin, minister of the Shawmut Avenue Universalist Church, organized a corporation to purchase it as a self-supporting residence for women. In the early 1970s it was converted to elderly housing.

☞ *Directions: Turn left on Washington Street to West Brookline Street.*

SE26: View of Holy Cross Cathedral High School and St. Helena's House

74 and 89 Union Park Street
The Sisters of St. Joseph have directed and staffed Cathedral High School since its founding in 1926 and the nearby Cathedral Grammar School since 1911. In addition to emphasizing academic excellence, the high school staff encourages their culturally diverse student body to participate in the school's sports, drama, and choral programs. The Sisters of St. Joseph operated St. Helena's House at 89 Union Park Street as housing for women who had just arrived in Boston. It was formerly the Grey Nuns Home for Working Girls and is now elderly housing.

☞ *Directions: Turn left on West Brookline Street to Shawmut Avenue.*

SE27: John Williams Municipal Building, former Little City Hall, and South End Branch Library

Corner of Shawmut and West Brookline Streets

One of the locations for community meetings supporting the creation of Villa Victoria was the John Williams Municipal Building. As the first woman mayor of the South End's Little City Hall, established by Mayor Kevin White in the 1970s, **Jeanette Hajjar** (1928–2004) worked to sustain community programs and institutions. Hajjar was a scholar of Middle Eastern studies and later served as a Peace Corps volunteer and an English teacher in Morocco.

☞ *Directions: Cross Shawmut and continue up West Brookline Street.*

Helen Morton (right) and Paula Oyola break the ceremonial ground for Villa Victoria

"Get involved: whether in one's immediate neighborhood in the affairs of one's city or town, in the nation, or the world! Thinking from the small to the large is exciting, like changing from microscope to telescope—all interrelated." —Helen Morton

SE28: Home of Helen Morton

83 West Brookline Street

The former home of **Helen Morton** (1898-1991) is now owned by the Salvation Army. Morton was a long-time South End activist, beginning with her service as a worker in the South End House in 1922 after she graduated from the Simmons College School of Social Work. In 1945, she helped with post war restoration in Europe. She returned in 1949 as associate head worker of the South End House and later as woman's worker for nearby St. Stephen's Church. Morton changed from a social worker to a political activist during the 1960s when she joined the effort to create Villa Victoria out of the city's Parcel 19. She and **Paula Oyola** (see SE29) were the two women chosen to break the ceremonial ground for Villa Victoria.

☞ *Directions: Return to Shawmut Avenue and turn left.*

SE29: Villa Victoria Cultural Center, Inquilinos Boricuas en Accion (IBA) and Paula Oyola, Latina activist

405 Shawmut Avenue

Latino community residents founded Inquilinos Boricuas en Accion (IBA) in 1968 to develop and now maintain Villa Victoria, a subsidized housing community built on a parcel of city land slated for urban renewal. IBA promotes the social and economic well being of Villa Victoria's residents with programs that support the arts, especially expressing the Latino cultural and artistic heritage. IBA offers intergenerational activities, programs for elders, educational initiatives, and job training.

Among the Latina activists was **Paula Oyola** (1917-2004), who was born in Puerto Rico, the ninth of eleven children.

Villa Victoria, where the Inquilinos Boricuas en Accion (IBA) promotes the social and economic well being of residents, as well as the arts.

Although she left school after the second grade to help on her family's farm, she taught herself to read and write with the help of her grandmother. In 1961, then the widowed mother of five, she moved to the United States and settled in the South End. She enjoyed introducing people to Puerto Rican culture. She said, "If you learn to dance salsa, you can dance anything." Once Villa Victoria was on its way, Oyola traveled to cities in Texas, California, and Florida helping to empower Latinos to fight urban renewal plans that would force them out of their neighborhoods.

☞ *Directions: Continue on Shawmut Avenue. On the right, note the Blackstone Public School, a Boston elementary school. Turn left on West Dedham Street, noting the community garden called the Unity Towers Garden with its sign in three languages. Walk to the Villa Victoria sign.*

SE30: Myrna Vazquez and Villa Victoria Center
West Dedham Street
Signs in the center of Villa Victoria illustrate community pride. One of the founders of Villa Victoria was **Myrna Vazquez** (1935–75), a renowned actress in Puerto Rico who had a lasting influence on the community. Although she lived in the South End only during the last year of her life, she was a charismatic political activist who combined art and action and helped found the IBA art component and the annual Puerto Rican Festival. Casa Myrna Vazquez, New England's largest shelter for battered women, is named for her.

Myrna Vazquez

☞ *Directions: Continue up West Dedham Street to Tremont Street; turn right. Turn right onto Union Park.*

SE31: South End House Site
20 Union Park
One of the first branches of the South End House was 20 Union Park (see SE22). It began as a men's residence in 1901, and later became a service center until 1959. **Beatrice Williams** (1898–1986) lived and served the community in this South End House residence for twenty-five years. She represented the South End on many city commissions. She began her lifetime of service in 1920 when she worked in France as a member of the American Committee for Devastated France helping with the restoration of twenty-six villages in northern France destroyed during the first World War.

☞ *Directions: Return to Tremont Street; turn right.*

SE32: Boston Center for the Arts
539 Tremont Street
E. Virginia Williams of the Boston Ballet
19 Clarendon Street

The Cyclorama building, the centerpiece of the Boston Center for the Arts, has a long history since it opened in 1884 to huge circular displays of historic scenes. Now adapted to the many activities of the BCA, its main hall has been the space for many events including opera impresario **Sarah Caldwell's** performance of *Louise* in 1980 (see C3) and artist **Judy Chicago's** exhibition, *Dinner Party*, in 1990. A lower floor includes three small theaters, the Community Music Center (see SE22), and the Boston Ballet Costume Shop. The BCA's goal is to "connect arts to the community" by supporting working artists "to create, perform, and exhibit new work." Its complex of buildings includes studio and rehearsal space for artists in the old Smith Organ building. It is a co-sponsor with Boston University of the Huntington Theater Company's new theater named for **Virginia Wimberly** (1936–2004), a piano teacher and philanthropist.

One of the newest buildings in the BCA complex is the Boston Ballet Building opened in 1991. The founder of the Boston Ballet in 1963 was **E. Virginia Williams** (1914–84), a dynamic leader and artist. A dancer herself, Williams chose to devote her life to creating the first professional repertory ballet company in New England. Under Williams's leadership and those of her successors, the company is now one of the top five ballet companies in North America. Upon the recommendation of choreographer

George Balanchine, Virginia Williams started the Boston Ballet with a large Ford Foundation grant, changing its name from the New England Civic Ballet Company. The Boston Ballet's official debut was on January 25, 1965, in John Hancock Hall. Committed to developing new generations of dancers, Williams's dance education program has grown to become the Center for Dance Education. It includes the Boston Ballet School, summer dance programs, Citydance, and Taking Steps. The Ballet's *Nutcracker* is an essential part of Boston's annual holiday celebration. The Boston Ballet tours internationally, and, when in Boston, its audiences fill the theaters.

☞ *Directions: To return to Back Bay Station, continue down Clarendon Street.*

> *"The Company Williams eventually formed and nurtured became the embodiment of her belief in both the art form and its artists. Williams chose to focus on the success of Boston Ballet rather than her own dance career. As a result of her selflessness, Boston Ballet grew to reflect not only the unrelenting determination of a notoriously driven woman, but also the unyielding power of a dynamic art form. Under Williams, Boston Ballet attracted many individuals, who devoted their lives to the creation of an ever-changing yet brilliantly cohesive dance company."*
> —Boston Ballet

Credits

Title page: courtesy of Susan Wilson.

Page 9: photo by Susan Wilson.

Page 10: postcard produced by the Mass. Foundation for the Humanities.

Page 11: courtesy of The Boston Athenæum.

Page 12: top: photo by Susan Wilson; bottom: courtesy of The Bostonian Society/Old State House.

Page 13: courtesy of the Schlesinger Library, Radcliffe Institute for Advanced Study, Harvard University.

Page 14: top: courtesy of the Fogg Art Museum, Harvard University; bottom: courtesy of the Christian Science Publishing Society.

Page 15: top: courtesy of Polly Welts Kaufman; bottom: courtesy of Dr. John Duff.

Page 16: top: courtesy of the Schlesinger Library, Radcliffe Institute; bottom: courtesy of the Peabody Essex Museum, Salem, Mass.

Page 17: top: courtesy of the Massachusetts Historical Society; bottom: bequest of Winslow Warren, courtesy of the Museum of Fine Arts, Boston.

Page 18: courtesy of the University of Nebraska.

Page 19: top: courtesy of the Museum of Fine Arts, Boston; bottom: photo by Susan Wilson.

Page 20: top: courtesy of the Perkins School for the Blind; bottom: courtesy of The Bostonian Society/Old State House.

Page 21: top left: courtesy of The Bostonian Society/Old State House; top right: courtesy of Susan Wilson; bottom: courtesy of The Bostonian Society/Old State House.

Page 22: courtesy of The Bostonian Society/Old State House.

Page 23: courtesy of the Terra Foundation for American Art.

Page 25: courtesy of the Boston Public Library.

Page 26: courtesy of Suzanne Spencer-Wood.

Page 27: top: courtesy of the Langone family; bottom: courtesy of the Museum of Fine Arts, Boston.

Page 28: top: photo by Susan Wilson; bottom: courtesy of The Bostonian Society/Old State House.

Page 29: top: courtesy of the Andover-Harvard Theological Library, Harvard University; bottom: courtesy of the Schlesinger Library, Radcliffe Institute.

Page 30: top: courtesy of Historic New England, Inc. (formerly the Society for the Preservation of New England Antiquities); bottom: courtesy of Kate Clifford Larson.

Page 31: top: courtesy of the Schlesinger Library, Radcliffe Institute. bottom: courtesy of Temple Israel Archives.

Page 33: photo by Susan Wilson.

Page 34: left: courtesy of The Boston Athenæum; right: courtesy of the Nichols House Museum.

Page 35: left: courtesy of the New England School of Law; right: courtesy of the Peabody Essex Museum.

Page 36: top: courtesy of the Boston Public Library; bottom: photo by Susan Wilson.

Page 37: photo by Susan Wilson.

Page 38: left: courtesy of Susan Wilson; right: courtesy of the Schomburg Center for Black Culture.

Page 39: top: courtesy of Dorothy Sterling from *Black Foremothers*; bottom: photo by Susan Wilson.

Page 40: courtesy of Wellesley College Archives.

Page 41: courtesy of the Afro American Studies Center, Boston University.
Page 43: courtesy of the Schlesinger Library, Radcliffe Institute.
Page 44: courtesy of the *Boston Globe*.
Page 45: left: courtesy of the Boston Public Library;
    right: courtesy of the Chin family.
Page 46: scan from microfilm, *Boston Globe*.
Page 47: courtesy of the Maryknoll Mission Archives.
Page 48: all: courtesy of the Schlesinger Library, Radcliffe Institute.
Page 49: top: courtesy of Chinese Historical Society; bottom: photo by Susan Wilson.
Page 50: courtesy of the International Brotherhood of Electrical Workers.
Page 51: courtesy of the Women's Educational and Industrial Union.
Page 52: photo by Susan Wilson.
Page 53: illustration by Karen Tenney.
Page 54: courtesy of Virginia Eskin.
Page 55: courtesy of Ginny O'Neil.
Page 56: courtesy of the Simmons College Archives.
Page 57: top: courtesy of the Boston Public Library;
    bottom: courtesy of the Museum of Fine Arts, Boston.
Page 59: courtesy of the Isabella Stewart Gardner Museum.
Page 60: photo by Susan Wilson.
Page 61: both: courtesy of The Schlesinger Library, Radcliffe Institute.
Page 63: photo by Susan Wilson.
Page 64: photo by Jeff Johnson.
Page 67: top left: courtesy of the Cass family;
    bottom right: courtesy of the Sophia Smith Collection, Smith College.
Page 68: top left: courtesy of the Boston Public Library;
    bottom right: courtesy of the Vassar College Library.
Page 70: top left: courtesy of the Junior League of Boston;
    right: photo by Judith Sedwick, courtesy of Ben Wallace.
Page 73: photo by Susan Wilson.
Page 75: photo by Susan Wilson.
Page 76: top: courtesy of The Schlesinger Library, Radcliffe Institute;
    bottom: photo by Susan Wilson.
Page 77: photo by Susan Wilson.
Page 78: left: courtesy of Polly Welts Kaufman; right: courtesy of South End Historical Society.
Page 79: scanned from *A Salute to Woman* (Women's Service Club, 1980).
Page 80: courtesy of the New England Conservatory.
Page 81: public domain photograph
Page 82: Cambridge Public Library collection, Cambridge Historical Commission.
Page 83: courtesy of Bethany Union.
Page 84: courtesy of Boston University Medical Center.
Page 85: courtesy of South End Historical Society.
Page 86: top left: courtesy of South End Historical Society;
    top right, bottom right: courtesy of the Saquet family.
Page 87: courtesy of South End Historical Society.
Page 88: courtesy of South End Historical Society.
Page 89: left: photo by Susan Wilson;
    right: courtesy of the Vazquez family.
Page 98: photo by Linda Haas.
Page 102: photo by Susan Wilson.
Page 105: courtesy of the Boston Public Library.
Page 107: photo by Michelle Jenney.

Full map: 2006 © Bruce Jones Design, Inc.
  modifications and individual maps: Bonnie Hurd Smith

Boston Area Research Resources

The Archives for Women In Medicine
A Project of the Joint Committee
on the Status of Women and the
Countway Library (Harvard
Medical School)
www.countway.harvard.edu/rarebooks/
awm.shtml

The Boston Athenæum
10 1/2 Beacon Street
Boston, MA 02108
617-227-0270
www.bostonathenaeum.org

Boston Public Library
666 Boylston Street
Boston, MA 02116
617-536-5400
www.bpl.org

The Bostonian Society
15 State Street
Boston, MA 02108
617-720-3285
www.bostonhistory.org

Jewish Women's Archive
138 Harvard Street
Brookline, MA 02446
617-232-2258
www.jwa.org

Massachusetts Historical Society
1154 Boylston Street
Boston, MA 02215
617-536-1608
www.masshist.org

Museum of Fine Arts, Boston
465 Huntington Avenue
Boston, MA 02115
617-267-9300
www.mfa.org

New England Historic Genealogical Society (NEHGS)
101 Newbury Street
Boston, MA 02116
617-536-5740
www.nehgs.org

The Schlesinger Library
Radcliffe Institute for Advanced
Study, Harvard University
10 Garden Street
Cambridge, MA 02138
617-495-8647
www.radcliffe.edu/schles/

Historic New England, Inc.
(formerly SPNEA)
141 Cambridge Street
Boston, MA 02114
617-227-3956
www.historicnewengland.org

State House Archives
State House, Room 33
Boston, MA 02133
617-727-2816
www.sec.state.ma.us/arc/arccol/colidx.htm

Unitarian Universalist Women's Heritage Society
Bethany Union
256 Newbury Street
Boston, MA 02116
www.uuwhs.org

More About Boston Women

A Selected List

Books

Alcott, Louisa May. *Hospital Sketches*. Bessie Z. Jones, ed.,
Harvard University Press, 1960.

Antin, Mary. *The Promised Land*. Houghton Mifflin, 1912; Penguin Classics, 1997.

Blanchard, Paula. *Margaret Fuller: From Transcendentalism to Revolution*.
Addison-Wesley, 1987.

Butterfield, Lyman H., et. al., eds. *The Book of Abigail and John: Selected Letters,
1762-1784*. Harvard University Press, 1975.

Cleary, Patricia. *Elizabeth Murray: A Woman's Pursuit of Independence in
Eighteenth-century America*. University of Massachusetts Press, 2000.

Clifford, Deborah. *Mine Eyes Have Seen the Glory: A Biography
of Julia Ward Howe*. Little, Brown, 1979.

Crawford, Deborah. *Four Women in a Violent Time* [Anne Hutchinson and
Mary Dyer]. Crown Publishers, 1970.

Cromwell, Adelaide M. *The Other Brahmins: Boston's Black Upper
Class*, 1750-1950. University of Arkansas Press, 1994.

Davidson, Margaret. *Helen Keller's Teacher* [Annie Sullivan]. Scholastic, 1996.

Deutsch, Sarah. *Women and the City: Gender, Space, and Power in Boston,
1870-1940*, Oxford University Press, 2000.

Drachman, Virgina B. *Hospital with a Heart: Women Doctors and the Paradox of
Separatism and the New England Hospital, 1862-1969*. Cornell University Press, 1984.

Dykeman, Therese Boos. *American Women Philosophers, 1650-1930: Six Exemplary
Thinkers* [Mercy Otis Warren, Judith Sargent Murray, Ednah Dow Cheney].
Edwin Mellon Press, 1993.

Elbert, Sarah. *A Hunger for Home: Louisa May Alcott's Place in American Culture.* Rutgers University Press, 1987.

Fairbanks, Henry G. *Louise Imogen Guiney: Laureate of the Lost.* Magi Books, 1972.

Faxon, Alicia and Moore, Sylvia, eds. *Pilgrims and Pioneers: New England Women in the Arts* [Charlotte Cushman, Harriet Hosmer, Edmonia Lewis, Anne Whitney]. Midmarch Arts Press, 1987.

Freedman, Florence B. *Two Tickets to Freedom: The True Story of Ellen and William Craft*, Fugitive Slaves. B. Bedrick, 1971.

Gamber, Wendy. *The Female Economy: The Millinery and Dressmaking Trades, 1865-1930.* University of Illinois Press, 1997.

Gates, Henry Louis Jr. *The Trials of Phillis Wheatley: America's First Black Poet and Encounters with the Founding Fathers.* Basic Civitas, 2003.

Gibran, Jean and Kahlil. *Kahlil Gibran, His Life and World.* Interlink, rev. ed. 1993.

Gill, Gillian. *Mary Baker Eddy.* Perseus Books, 1998.

Goldfarb, Hilliard T. *The Isabella Stewart Gardner Museum: A Companion Guide and History.* Yale University Press, 1995.

Golin, Rita K. *Annie Adams Fields, Woman of Letters.* University of Massachusetts Press, 2002.

Gollaher, David L. *Voice for the Mad: The Life of Dorothea Dix.* Free Press, 1995.

Graham, Shirley. *The Story of Phillis Wheatley.* Julian Messner, 1949.

Guerrier, Edith. *An Independent Woman: The Autobiography of Edith Guerrier.* Molly Matson, ed. University of Massachusetts Press, 1992.

Hansen, Debra Gold. *Strained Sisterhood: Gender and Class in the Boston Female Anti-Slavery Society.* University of Massachusetts Press, 1993.

Higginbotham, Evelyn Brooks. *Righteous Discontent: The Women's Movement in the Black Baptist Church, 1880-1920.* Harvard University Press, 1993.

Hirshler, Erica. *A Studio of Her Own: Women Artists in Boston, 1879-1940.* Museum of Fine Arts, Boston, 2001.

Humez, Jean M. *Harriet Tubman: The Life and the Life Stories.* University of Wisconsin Press, 2003.

Kaufman, Polly Welts. *Boston Women and City School Politics, 1872-1905.* Garland Publishing, Inc., 1994.

Kerr, Andrea Moore. *Lucy Stone: Speaking Out for Equality.* Rutgers University Press, 1992.

La Plante, Eve. *American Jezebel: The Uncommon Life of Anne Hutchinson, the Woman Who Defied the Puritans.* HarperSanFrancisco, 2004.

Lerner, Gerda. *The Grimke Sisters from South Carolina: Pioneers for Women's Rights and Abolition.* Schocken Books, 1967.

Marshall, Megan. *The Peabody Sisters: Three Women Who Ignited American Romanticism.* Houghton Mifflin Co., 2005.

Mason, James D. Jr., ed. *The Poems of Phillis Wheatley.* University of North Carolina Press, 1989.

Merrill, Marlene Deahl, ed. *Growing Up in Boston's Gilded Age: The Journal of Alice Stone Blackwell, 1872-1874.* Yale University Press, 1990.

Morton, Helen. *Highlights: 80 Years Worth Living.* Kennebec River Press, 1990.

Nolan, Janet. *Servants of the Poor: Teachers and Mobility in Ireland and Irish America.* University of Notre Dame Press, 2004.

Norwood, Stephen H. *Labor's Flaming Youth: Telephone Operators and Worker Militancy, 1878-1923.* University of Illinois Press, 1990.

Paul, Susan. *Memoir of James Jackson.* Lois Brown, ed. Harvard University Press, 2000.

Porter, Susan, ed. *Women of the Commonwealth: Work, Family, and Social Change in Nineteenth Century Massachusetts.* [Julia Harrington Duff, Emily Greene Balch, Josephine St. Pierre Ruffin] University of Massachusetts Press, 1996.

Richardson, Marilyn, ed. *Maria W. Stewart, America's First Black Woman Political Writer.* Indiana University Press, 1987.

Richmond, Merle. *Phillis Wheatley: Poet.* Chelsea House, 1988.

Roman, Judith A. *Annie Adams Fields: The Spirit of Charles Street.* Indiana University Press, 1990.

Ronda, Bruce. *Elizabeth Palmer Peabody: A Reformer On Her Own Terms.* Harvard Univeristy Press, 1999.

Shakir, Evelyn. *Bint Arab: Arab and Arab American Women in the United States.* Praeger, 1997.

Smith, Bonnie Hurd. *The Letters I Left Behind: Judith Sargent Murray Papers, Letter Book 10.* Judith Sargent Murray Society, 2006.

Stern, Madeleine B. *Louisa May Alcott.* University of Oklahoma Press, 1950.

Strom, Sharon Hartman. *Political Woman: Florence Luscomb and the Legacy of Radical Reform.* Harvard University Press, 2001.

Taylor, Susie King. *A Black Woman's Civil War Memoirs.* Patricia W. Romero and Willie Lee Rose, eds. Markus Weiner Publishing, 1988.

Van Doren, Carl. *Jane Mecom: Benjamin Franklin's Favorite Sister.* Augustus M. Kelly, 1973.

Venet, Wendy Hamand. *A Strong-Minded Woman: The Life of Mary Livermore.* University of Massachusetts Press, 2005.

Waterston, Anna Cabot Lowell Quincy. *A Woman's Wit & Whimsy: The 1833 Diary of Anna Cabot Lowell Quincy.* Beverly Wilson Palmer, ed., Northeastern University Press, 2003.

Wheeler, Leslie, ed. *Loving Warriors: Selected Letters of Lucy Stone and Henry B. Blackwell, 1853 to 1893.* Dial Press, 1981.

Wilson, Susan. *Boston Sites and Insights.* Beacon Press, 2003.

Wilson, Susan. *The Literary Trail of Greater Boston.* Commonwealth Editions, 2005.

Wilson, Susan. *Garden of Memories: A Guide to Historic Forest Hills.* Forest Hills Educational Trust, 1998.

Reference
Notable American Women: A Biographical Dictionary.
Vol. 1-3: Edward T. and Janet James, eds., Harvard University Press, 1971. Vol. 4: Barbara Sicherman and Carol Hurd Green, eds., Harvard University Press, 1980. Vol. 5, Susan Ware, ed., Stacy Braukman, asst. ed., Harvard University Press, 2004.

Acknowledgments

Our most sincere thanks to: Kathy Amico, Donna Baines, Martha Bartle, Emilie Beattie, Ellen Berrahmoun, Eugene Boehne, Webster Bull, Richard O. Card, Joanne Ciccarello, Sharlene Cochrane, Lorna Condon, Christopher Conway, Norma Corey, Stephen Dickerman, Lydia Dufour, Rev. Dorothy May Emerson, Jovita Fontanez, Clara Garcia, Marie-Helene Gold, Sandy Goldsmith, Claire Goodwin, Joan W. Goodwin, Matt Greif, Pamela Greiff, Denise Hajjar, Clare and Chris Hayes, Mary and Bernard Hayes, Yvonne Homsy, Janet Howell, Betsy Johnson, Kyle Johnson, Joyce King, Carolyn Kirdahy, David Lapin, Kate Clifford Larson, Thomas Loring, Bill Meikle, Cheryl Moneyhun, Sister Cathy Mozzicato CSJ, David Nathan, John Neale, Kate Ohno, Susan M. Olsen, Karen L. Otis, Bob Pessek, Aleta K. Pinard, Susan Porter, Michael Prodanou, Katherine Rawlins, Jean Rees, Paula Richter, Robert Saquet, Aaron Schmidt, Jon Seamans, Evelyn Shakir, Sister Therezon Sheerin CSJ, Wilma Slaight, Doug Southard, Suzanne Spencer-Wood, Chris Steele, Cynthia Stone, Matt Strobel, Charles Sullivan, Kristen Swett, Karen Tenney, Theresa Tirella, Paul Wright.

The Board of Directors of the Boston Women's Heritage Trail acknowledges, in particular, the generous and ongoing support of the City of Boston, Thomas M. Menino, Mayor, and the Boston Women's Commission; and the Boston Public Schools, Thomas Payzant, Superintendent.

Our generous funder for this third edition:
The Cabot Family Charitable Trust

Blackstone School students celebrate the opening of their year-long project:
the South End Women's Heritage Trail

Sister Trails

Remembering the Ladies:
A South Shore Women's Heritage Trail
(published by the Patriot Ledger, Quincy, MA
available at www.bwht.org)

Salem Women's Heritage Trail
Salem Maritime National Historic Site Visitor Center
East India Square, Salem, MA 01970
(www.swht.org)

Unitarian Universalist Women's History Walking Tour
Unitarian Universalist Women's Heritage Society
Bethany Union
256 Newbury Street, Boston, MA 02116
(www.uuwhs.org)

Women's History Heritage Trail
Worcester Women's History Project
30 Elm Street, Worcester, MA 01609
(www.wwhp.org)

Women's History Walking Trail in Brunswick, Maine
Pejepscot Historical Society
159 Park Row, Brunswick, ME 04011
(wwwcurtislibrary.com/pejepscot.htm)

Women's History Walking Trail in Portland, Maine
Department of History,
University of Southern Maine
P.O. Box 9300, Portland, ME 04104
(www.USM.Maine.edu/~history/newtrail.html)

"...men are called on from an early period to reproduce all that they learn. Their college exercises, their political duties, their professional studies...call on them to put to use what they have learned. But women learn without any attempt to reproduce. Their only reproduction is for purposes of display. It is to supply this defect that these conversations have been planned." —Margaret Fuller

Index

A Better Chance (ABCD), 81
Abiel Smith School, 36
abolition/abolitionists, 14, 22, 36, 37, 39.
   See also anti-slavery.
Academy of Musical Arts, 79
actors/actresses, 12, 13, 14, 21-22, 26, 29, 63
Adams, Abigail, site of, 16-17; statue of, 73
Adams, Hannah, 12
Adams, John, 16-17
Adams, Sam, statue of, 18, 40
Addams, Jane, 67
African American Community, 14, 16, 20, 35,
   36-37, 39, 40-41, 50-51, 56-57, 66.
   See also Abolition, African Meeting House,
   Anti-Slavery, Underground Railroad
African Meeting House, site of, 36
Alcott, Anna B., 83
Alcott, Bronson, 35
Alcott, Louisa May, 10, 40, 83, site of, 35-36.
   See also Louisa May Alcott Club and School.
Alexander, Jane, 69
Allen, Tina, 75
American Academy of Arts and Sciences, 59,
   site of, 68
American Association of University Women, 54
American Nurses Association, 36-38
American Peace Society, 66
American Revolution, 16-17, 22, 27
American Woman Suffrage Association, 12, 14
anti-slavery, American Anti-Slavery Society, 22;
   bazaars/fairs, 18, 22; Female (and Boston)
   Anti-Slavery Society, 14, 22, 37, 39;
   petitions, 11;
anti-war movement. See peace movement.
Antin, Mary, 63, 86
Appleton Street School, 76
Archeologists, 82
Arab-American community, 46-47, 86-87
Arrington, Geneva, 79
artists, 34, 49, 51, 57, 71-72. See also sculptors.
Arts and Crafts Movement, 30, 72
Associated Charities of Boston, 41
Association for the Advancement of Women,
   14, 58, 69
astronomers, 68-69
athletes, 64-65
attorneys, 34-35, 44
aviators, 48, 49

Back Bay Station, site of, 75
Back Bay Stompers, 80

Balanchine, George, 90
Balch, Emily Greene, site of, 61
Baldwin, Maria Louise, 82
Barron, Jennie Loitman, site of, 16
Barton, Clara, 10-11
Batson, Ruth, 36
Bauer, Margaret H., 35
Beach, Amy, site of, 54
Beach, Dr. Henry Harris, 54
Beal, Elizabeth Sturgis Grew, 54
Beaux, Cecelia, 71
Bergmann, Meredith, 73
Berlin, Viola and Florence, 72
Bethany Home for Young Women, site of, 83
Bethune, Mary McLeod, 78
Bickerdyke, Mother, 55
Blackwell, Alice Stone, 12, 64; bust of, 65
Blackwell, Henry, 12, 65
Boston Art Students Association, 57
Boston Athenæum, site of, 11
Boston Ballet, 90
Boston Center for the Arts, site of, 90
Boston Center for Adult Education, site of, 57
Boston City Hospital, 18
Boston Equal Suffrage Association for
   Good Government, 65
Boston Latin School, 85.
   See also Girls Latin School.
Boston Marathon, site of, 64-65
"Boston marriage," 40
Boston Massacre, 16
Boston Municipal Court, 16
Boston Normal School, 15, 76, 85
Boston Pops, 79
Boston Public Library, 30, 40, 86; site of, 63
Boston Public Schools, 15, 31, 16, 37, 41, 47,
   68, 70
Boston Public School teachers, 15, 41, 47, 76, 82
Boston School Committee, 15-16, 23, 78, 84, 85
Boston School Committeewomen, site of, 15
Boston Society of Natural History, 67
Boston State College, 76
Boston Symphony Orchestra, 54
Boston Tea Party, 17. See also New England
   Women's Tea Party.
Boston Teachers College, 76
Boston University, 37, 65. 79; School of
   Medicine, 79, 84
Boston Women's Health Collective, 51
Boston Women's Memorial, 12, 17, 20, 46;
   site of, 73

Boston Women's Trade Union League,
site of, 50. *See also* Women's Trade Union
League.
Bradley, Susan Hinckley, 66
Braxton, Blanche Woodson, 35
Briggs, Luther, Jr., 82
Brimmer School, 60
Brodney, Edward, 10
Brodney, Sarah, 10
Brooks, Reverend Phillips, 66
Brotherhood of Sleeping Car Porters, 75
Brown, Edith, 30
Brown, Margaret Fitzhugh, 71
Bulfinch, Charles, 23, 29, 33
Bunker Hill Monument, 18, 28
Bush-Brown, Lydia, 72
Business women, 13, 19, 50-51, 56

Caldwell, Sarah, 90, site of, 44
Cambridge School (Cambridge School
at Weston), 60
Cass, Melnea, 64, 66-67, 81-82
Cassatt, Mary, 57, 71
Cathedral High School, 87-88.
See also Holy Cross Cathedral.
Center for Dance, 90
Chiang Kai Shek, Madame, 45
Chapman, Maria Weston, 22, 39
Channing, William Ellery, 22
Charles Street A.M.E. Church, 41
Chase, Adelaide Cole, 71
Cheney, Ednah Dow Littlehale, 43, 67, 84
Chester Square, site of, 82
Chiang, Judy, 90
Child, Abby, 69
Child, Lydia Maria, 22
Children's Art Centre, 81; site of, 84-85
Children's Friend Society, 85
Chilton, Mary. *See* Winslow, Mary Chilton.
Chin, Chew Shee, 45
Chinatown Community Mural, site of, 49
Chinese-American Civic Association, 47
Chinese-American community, 45-49
Chippewas, 14
Chrimes, Louise, 72
Christian Science Church. See Church of Christ,
Scientist.
Church, Dr. Adeline, 84
Church of Christ, Scientist, 15, 80
Church of the Covenant, site of, 69
City Dance, 90
civil rights movement, 40-41, 50-51, 66, 70-71
Civil War, 10-12, 34, 36, 76-77; 54th
Massachusetts Regiment,12-14; Civil War
Nurse Memorial, 10
clergy: African Americans as, 36-37, 39;

challenges to established, 9-10, 15, 28;
women as, 15, 69
Clisby, Dr. Harriet, 51
Coeducation. *See* education.
College Club, site of, 54
College Equal Suffrage Association, 64
College Settlement House Association, 48
Collins, Patrick, statue of, 55, 73
Colored American, 51
Commonwealth Avenue Mall, 55, 72-73
Community gardens, 87, 89. *See also* Unity
Towers Garden.
Community Music Center, 85, 90
Compagnion, Yvette, 73
composers, and conductors, 21-22, 44, 54, 90
Cooper, Hattie B., 78
Copley Society of Boston, 57, site of, 71
Craft, Ellen and William, 37; site of, 39
crafts, 26, 48, 51, 72. *See also* Arts and Crafts
Movement and Paul Revere Pottery.
Crawford, Winifred, 72
Crittendon Women's Union, 51
Crocker, Lucretia, 15, 67, 68, site of, 78
Crosby, Estella, site of, 79
Crosson, Wilhelmina, 82
Crumpler, Dr. Arthur, 37
Crumpler, Dr. Rebecca Lee, 84, site of, 37
Cunningham, Fern, 77
Cushman, Charlotte, 14, 26, 29, 40, 63
Cyclorama Building, 90

Dallin, Cyrus E., 9
dancers, 79, 80, 89, 90
Dane, Francis and Zervia, 82
Daughters of Charity, 64
Davenport, Mildred, site of, 79
Davis, Mary E.P., 38
de Bretteville, Sheila Levrant, 10
Deland, Margaret, site of, 40
Delta sigma theta, 84
Denison House, 51, 85, site of, 48
desegregation, 36, 66, 70-71
Dewing, Carolyn L., 70
Dimock Community Health Center, 38
discrimination, 76, 79
Dix, Dorothea, site of, 10-11
doctors, 29, 37, 38, 51, 84
Doriot, Edna, 58
Dressmakers, 13, 51. *See also* garment workers.
Dress Reform Parlors, site of, 13
Drown, Lucy Lincoln, 18
Dudley, Helena, 48
Duff, Julia Harrington, 15
Durant, Pauline, 66
Dyer, Mary, 28, 33; site and statue of, 9-10

Earhart, Amelia, 48
Easter Parade, 55
Eddy, Mary Baker, 64; sites of, 14-15, 80
editors, 12, 14, 34, 40, 65; site of women
    editors, 50
education, adult, 57; art, 70-72, 79, 80;
    coeducation, 13, 47, 63-69, 84, 85;
    dance, 79, 80; female academies, 21, 23;
    higher, 12, 54, 55-56, 60, 67-69, 78;
    independent schools for girls, site of, 60-61;
    handicapped, 20; kindergartens, 26, 30, 35, 44;
    legal, 34-35; medical, 38, 84; science, 67-68;
    78; vocational, 30-31, 56-57, 66-68, 70, 72,
    73, 81. *See also* Boston School Committee,
    Boston Public Schools, desegregation, Girls
    Latin School.
Ellis Memorial Center, 81
Elma Lewis School of Fine Arts. *See* Lewis, Elma.
Emancipation (sculpture), 77
Emerson College, 66-67, 70; site of, 56-57
Emerson, Ralph Waldo, 44
environmentalists, 58, 67
Ericsson, Leif, statue of, 40, 73
Exeter Street Theater, site of, 72

464 Follies, 79-80
Fairmont Copley Plaza Hotel, 65
Faneuil Hall, site of, 18
fashion design, 70
Federal Street Church, site of, 22
Federal Street Theatre, site of, 21
Fenway Court. *See* Isabella Stewart Gardner.
Fichter, David, 49
Fields, Annie Adams, 12, 19, 41
Fields, James T., 19, 41
Fisher College, site of, 60
Fiske, Gertrude, 71
Fitzgerald, John F., 25
Fleet, Thomas, 14
Follen, Eliza Lee Cabot, 22
Foo, Ruby, site of, 46
Forest Hills Cemetery, 77
Franklin, Abiah, 13
Franklin, Benjamin, 13, 21
Franklin Place/Tontine Crescent, site of, 23
Franklin Square House, site of, 87
Freedom House, 70, 81
French Library and Cultural Center, site of, 58
Froebel, Frederick, 35
Fuller, Margaret, 43
Fuller, Meta Vaux Warrick, 71, 77, 84
Fuller, Solomon Carter, 77. *See also* Solomon
    Carter Fuller Center.
funeral directors, 76

Statue of Mary Dyer by Sylvia Shaw Judson
(see pages 9-10)

Garcia, Frieda, 85
Gardner, Anna Bobbitt, Academy of Musical
    Arts, site of, 79
Gardner, Eliza Endicott Peabody, 56
Gardner, George, 56
Gardner, Isabella Stewart, 56; site of, 59
Gardner, John L., 56
Gardner Museum. *See* Gardner, Isabella Stewart.
garment workers/industry, 45, 47, 49
Garrison, William Lloyd, 14, 22, 37, 39;
    sculptures of, 14, 40
General Federation of Women's Clubs, 58
Gibb, Roberta, 65
Gibbs College, *see* Katharine Gibbs School
Gibran, Kahlil, 60
Gibson, Betty, 82
Gibson, Charles Hammond, 59
Gibson House Museum (Catherine Hammond
    Gibson), site of, 59
Gibson, John Gardner, 59
Gibson, Rosamond Warren, 59-60
Girls High, 76, 86; site of, 85
Girls Latin School, 15, 23, 80; site of, 85
Glover, Goody, 26
Godey's Ladies Book, 28
Goldstein, Fanny, 30
Granary Burying Ground, site of, 13
Greater Boston Hotel and Restaurant
    Workers' Union, site of, 65
Green, Suzanne Revaleon, 15
Gregory, Dr. Samuel, 84
Grey Nuns, 87

Grimké, Angelina, 11
Grimké, Sarah, 11
Guerrier, Edith, 30
Guild of Boston Artists, site of, 71
Guiney, Louise Imogen, 41, 63, 79
Gussom, Gladys, 85
Hajjar, Jeanette, 88

Hageman, Alice, 69
Hale, Lillian Westcott, 71
Hale, Sarah Josepha, 18, 28
Hale House, 81
Hall, Harriet, 81
Hall, Minna, 58
Handel & Haydn Society, 54
handicapped people, 20
Hannon, Josephine, 28
Harriet Tubman House, sites of, 77, 81
Harriet Tubman Square, site of, 77
Hartnett, Ellen, 13
Haskell School for Girls (Mary Elizabeth
   Haskell), 60
Hastings, Dr. Caroline, 84
Hawes, Harriet Boyd, 82
Hawthorne, Nathaniel and Sophia, 44
Hayden, Harriet and Lewis, site of, 39
Hebrew Industrial School, site of, 31
Hebrew Ladies' Sewing Society, 31
Hecht, Lina, 31
Hecht Neighborhood House, 31
Hemenway, Harriet Lawrence, site of, 58
Hemenway, Mary Tileston, 20
Henson, Julia O., 77
Hirsch, Anna E., 35
historic preservation, 20, 27, 29, 34-35, 59, 67
Hi-Hat, 81
Hispanic community. See Latino community.
Holmes, Beatrix, 72
Holmes, Gladys, 82
Holocaust and Holocaust Memorial, 38,
   site of, 17-18
Holy Cross Cathedral, site of, 87-88
Homemakers Training Program, 81
homeopathy, 84
Hopkins, Pauline, 50-51
Hosmer, Harriet, 11, 29
Hotel and Restaurant Workers Union, 65
Housewives' League, 79
Howard Athenæum, site of, 16
Howard University Gallery of Art, 14
Howe, Julia Ward, 84; sites of, 33-34, 58-59
Howe, Samuel Gridley, 58
Hunt, Dr. Harriot Keziah, 29
Hutchinson, Anne, 19, 28, 33, 64; site and
   statue of, 9-10
Indian Rights Movement, 18.

See also Native American community.
Inquilinos Boricuas en Accion (IBA), 88-89
International Ladies Garment Workers Union,
   site of, 45
Irish-American community, 13, 15, 19-20, 25,
   26, 28, 44-45
Irish Famine Memorial, site of, 19
Italian-American community, 27, 30-31, 45, 83

Jackson, Helen Hunt, 18
Jencks, Penelope, 72
Jewett, Sarah Orne, 41
Jewish community, 17-18, 26, 30-31, 37-38, 83
Jordan, Alice M., 63
Joseph Lee School, 77
Judson, Sylvia Shaw, 10
judges, 35; site of women judges, 16
Junior League of Boston, site of, 69-70

Katharine Gibbs School, site of, 70
Kehew, Mary Morton, 51, 64
Keller, Helen, 19
Kennedy brothers: Joe Jr., John F., Robert, 25
Kennedy, Joseph, 25
Kennedy, Rose Fitzgerald, 29; sites of, 25, 28
kindergartens. See education.
King, Alice Spaulding and Henry, 60
King, Coretta Scott, 83
Kitson, Theo Ruggles and Henry Hudson, 55, 73
Kuscsik, Nina, 64

La Alianza Hispana, 85
labor movement, 12-13, 18, 44-45, 48, 50.
   See also trade unions.
Ladd, Anna Coleman, fountain by, 54
LaFlesche, Suzette "Bright Eyes," 18
Langone, Clementine Poto and Joseph Jr., 27
Lanyon, Ellen, 64
Latino community, 88-89
League of Women for Community Service,
   site of, 82-83
League of Women Voters, 16, 61, 65
Lebanese-Syrian Ladies' Aid Society, sites of, 46,
   86. See also Arab-American community.
LeFavour, Henry, 55
Lewis, Dr. Dio, 36
Lewis, Edmonia, 29; site of, 14
Lewis, Elma, and Elma Lewis School of
   Fine Arts, 56-57, 69
libraries, 11, 26, 63-64
Lincoln House, 81
Livermore, Mary Rice, 14
Little City Hall, 88
Lok, Rose, site of, 48-49
Longfellow, Henry Wadsworth, 14
Lorch, Grace Lonergan, 15

Louisa May Alcott Club, 83
Louisa May Alcott School, site of, 83
Lowell, Amy, 11
Lower, Donna Day, 69
Luscomb, Florence Hope, 10; site of, 61

MacLean, Bertha and Arthur W., 34
Macy, Annie Sullivan, 64, site of, 20
Mahan, Mary A., 44
Mahoney, Mary Eliza, site of, 38
Mann, Horace, 78, and Mary, 44
Manning, Adeline, 40
Mariners House, site of, 28
marriage laws, 15
Maryknoll Sisters of St. Dominic, site of, 47
Mason, Fanny and Peabody Mason Foundation,
    site of, 73
Massachusetts Anti-Suffragist Committee, 65
Massachusetts Association Opposed to the
    Further Extension of Suffrage to Women, 65
Massachusetts Audubon Society, site of, 58
Massachusetts Bar Association, site of, 44
Massachusetts College of Art, 72
Massachusetts Commission against
    Discrimination, 65, 79
Massachusetts Daughters of Veterans, 10
Massachusetts General Hospital, 56, site of, 38
Massachusetts Institute of Technology (MIT),
    Rogers Building, Woman's Laboratory,
    site of, 67
Massachusetts Library Association, 63
Massachusetts Men's League for Woman
    Suffrage, 65
Massachusetts Metaphysical College, 80
Massachusetts Normal Art School, 72
Massachusetts Nurses Association, 18
Massachusetts State Federation of
    Women's Clubs, 41
Massachusetts Woman Suffrage Association,
    58; site of, 65
May, Abby, 13, 15, 23, 67, 78, 84
The May School (Mary May), 61
McCluskey, Josephine, a.k.a. "Miss Delavenue,"
    13
McKay, Annie, 47
McKerrow, Cora Reed, site of 76
Mecom, Jane Franklin, 13; site of, 21
Meder, Elsa, 69
Menconi, Evelyn Abdalah, 87
mentally ill, advocacy for, 11
milliners, 51; site of, 13
missionaries, 39-40, 47
Mitchell, Lucy Miller, 66
Mitchell, Maria, 68-69
Monet, Claude, 71
Moore, Mary, fountain by, 54

Morison, Samuel Eliot, statue of, 72
Morton, Helen, site of, 88
Mota, Rosa, 65
"Mother Goose." See Vergoose, Elizabeth.
Moulton, Louise Chandler, site of, 78
Murray, Elizabeth, site of, 19
Murray, Reverend John, 23, 28
Murray, Judith Sargent Stevens, 21, 28-29;
    site of, 23
Museum of African American History, 36
Museum of Fine Arts (and School of), 34, 57, 71
Museum of Natural History, site of, 67
Museum of Science, 68
musicians, 44, 54, 73, 79-80, 85, 90

9 to 5 Office Workers' Union, site of, 13
National Association for the Advancement
    of Colored People (NAACP), 65, 81
National Association of Colored Women, 41
National Center of Afro-American Artists, 57
National Federation of Afro-American
    Women, 41
Native American community, 14, 18
Negro History Week, 80
New England Chinese Women's Association,
    site of, 45
New England Conservatory of Music, 79-80,
    82, 87
New England Female Medical College, 37;
    site of, 84
New England Holocaust Memorial.
    See Holocaust Memorial
New England Hospital for Women and
    Children, 38, 84
New England Roundtable of Children's
    Librarians, 63
New England School of Law, 35, 50
New England Telephone Company, 44
New England Woman Suffrage Association,
    18, 58, 65
New England Women's Club, 12, 15, 34, 58, 69
New England Women's Tea Party, 18
New Era Club, 40-41
New York streets area, 86
Nichols House Museum (Rose Standish
    Nichols), site of, 34
Nine Notable Women of Boston (mural),
    site of, 64
Ninety-Nines, 49
Nobel Peace Prize, 61
North Bennet Street Industrial School, site of, 30
North End Union, site of, 26
Norwood, Rose Finkelstein, 50
Nourse, Annie Endicott, 85
nuns, 39-40, 47, 64, 87
Nurses Hall (State House), site of, 10

nurses, 10, 18, 36, 38, 47, 76
Nutcracker (ballet), 90

O'Connor, Julia. *See* Parker, Julia O'Connor.
O'Neil, Julia Oliver and family, 55
O'Sullivan, John F., 48
O'Sullivan, Mary Kenney, 10, 48
Oberlin College, 12
Old Corner Bookstore, site of, 19
Old St. Stephens Church, site of, 29
Old State House, 16, 21
Old South Meeting House, site of, 20-21
Olympics, 64
Omaha Indians, 18
Opera, 44, 90
Our Bodies Ourselves, 51
Oyola, Paula, 88

Paeff, Bashka, fountain by, 54
Page, Marie Danforth, 71
Palmer, Sophia, 38
Palmer Memorial Institute, 82
Papanti, Lorenzo, 59
Parker, Julia O'Connor, 44, 50
Parsons, Lucy, 80
Patrons of: art, 14, 57, 71-72; literature, 12, 19,
    41, 78
Paul Revere House, 27
Paul Revere Pottery and Library Club House,
    site of, 30. *See also* Saturday Evening Girls.
Paul, Susan, 37; site of, 39
Paul, Reverend Thomas, 39
Paulist Fathers, 13
Payne-Gaposchkin, Cecilia, 69
Peabody, Amelia, 71
Peabody, Elizabeth Palmer, sites of, 35
    and 43-44
Peabody, Mary, 44
Peabody, Sophia, 44
Peabody Mason Foundation. *See* Mason, Fanny
peace movement, 48, 61, 66
Perdue, Gladys Moore, site of, 80
Perin, Reverend George L., 87
Puerto Rican community, 98-99
Perkins School for the Blind, 20
Perry, Lilla Cabot, 71
philanthropists, 12, 18, 20, 26, 28, 30-31, 34,
    38, 40, 41, 47-48, 57, 68,
philosophers, 23, 43-44
playgrounds, 26
playwrights, 17, 21-22
poets, 11, 20, 23, 46, 57, 63
Pollard, Ann, 29
political campaigns, 15, 25, 61
Portia School of Law, 44, 50; site of, 34-35
Poto Family Grocery Store, site of, 27

Prendergast, Maurice, 57
Prince, Lucinda W., 56. *See also* Simmons
    College.
Prince School, 56
property owners, 34, 57
Public Garden, 53-54
public speakers, 11, 14-15, 18, 22, 56-57
Pulitzer Prize, 57

Quakerism, 9
Quincy, Anna Cabot Lowell. *See* Waterston.
Quincy, Mayor Josiah, 82
Quincy Market, 18
Quincy School, site of, 47

racial discrimination. *See* discrimination.
Radical Club, 34
Rand, Belle, P., 58
Randolph, A. Philip, statue of, 75
Redmond, Margaret, 66
Reid Funeral Home, site of, 76
religious orders/communities, 39-40, 47, 87
religious tolerance/reform, 9-10, 14-15, 28, 33
Remond, Sarah Parker, 10; site of, 16
restaurateurs and workers, 46, 65
Revere, Paul, 27
Revere, Rachel Walker, site of, 27
Revere, Sarah Orne, 27
Rice, Elizabeth, 69
Rice School, site of, 76
Ridley, Florida Ruffin, 41, 82
Rodriquez, Ana Maria, 85
Richards, Ellen Swallow, 64, 67
Richards, Linda, site of, 38
Ridley, Florida Ruffin, 41, 82
Riley, Eileen, 69
Robba, Fatama, 65
Roberts, Benjamin, 36
Roberts, Sara, 36
Roberts Brothers, 36
Robinson, Beryl, 63
Rodriquez, Ana Maria, 85
Rogers, Margaret, 72
Rogers, Mother Mary Joseph, 47
Rose Kennedy Greenway, site of, 25.
    See also Kennedy, Rose.
Ross, Marjorie Drake, 59-60
Rowson, Susanna Haswell, site of, 21
Rowson, William, 21
Ruffin, Josephine St. Pierre, 10, 82; site of, 40-41
Ruffin, George, Lewis, 41

Saarinen, Lillian Swann, fountain by, 54
Safford-Blake, Dr. Mary, 84
Sampson, Deborah, 22
Samuelson, Joan Benoit, 65

Saquet, Labeebee Hanna, 87
Sargent, John Singer, 12
Sarmiento, Domingo, statue of, 73
Saturday Evening Girls, site of, 30.
    See also Paul Revere Pottery.
Schön, Nancy, 53, 64
School of Fashion Design, site of, 70
School of Housekeeping, 56
scientists, 15, 64, 67-69, 78
Scudder, Vida, 48
sculptors, 9-11, 14, 29, 53-54, 55, 58, 71, 77
Seaman's Aid Society, 28
Sears, Joshua Montgomery, 57
Sears, Mary Crease, 72
Sears, Sarah Choate, 71, 72; site of, 57
Sellers, Susan, 10
settlement houses, 48, 77, 81, 83, 84, 88
Severance, Caroline, 34
Sexton, Anne Gray, 57
Shakir, Hannah Sabbagh, 46-47, 83, 84, 86
Shaw, Josephine H., 72
Shaw, Pauline Agassiz, 30-31, 68
Shaw, Robert Gould, 12, 14
Shure, Robert, 9
Sinesi, Isobel, 70
Silver Box Studio, 74
Simmons College (Graduate School of Social
    Work, Graduate School of Management,
    Prince School of Salesmanship), 88; site of,
    55-56
Sister Ann Alexis, 64
Sister Magdalen, 72
Sisters of St. Joseph, 87
Slanger, Frances, 10-11
Slavery, 20, 46,76, 77
Smith School. See Abiel Smith School.
Snowden, Muriel S., site of Muriel S. Snowden
    International High School, 70
Snowden, Otto, 70
social workers, 47, 51, 52, 55-56
Society of Arts and Crafts, 57; site of, 72
Society of the Descendants of Early New
    England Negroes, 41
Solomon Carter Fuller Center, 84
South End Historical Society, 82
South End House, 84-85, 89; site of, 88
South End Music School, 85
spiritualism, 72, 79
Spiritualist Temple, site of, 72
St. Gaudens, Augustus, 12
St. Helena House, 87
St. James Hotel, 87
St. Leonard's Church, site of, 31
St. Margaret's Convent, site of, 39-40
State House (Doric Hall, site of Nurses Hall,
    10-11; House Chamber and Committee

    rooms, 11, 12
Statues, 9-10, 18, 19, 33, 40, 53-55, 72, 73, 77;
    of named women: 9-10, 73, 77-78
Step on Board (Harriet Tubman statue), site of, 77
Stewart, Maria, 37
Stimson, Louise, 26, 64
Stone, Lucy, 10, 12-13, 40, 64, 65; statue or
    bust of, 18, 40, 63, 73
Storrow, Helen Osborne, 30
storytelling, 63
Stowe, Harriet Beecher, 41
Stuart, Gilbert, 34
suffrage. See woman suffrage.
Sullivan, Annie. See Macy, Annie Sullivan.
Swan, Hepzibah Clarke, 33-34
Symphony Hall, 80
Syrian-Lebanese Society. See Lebanese-Syrian
    Society

Taylor, E. Alice, 79
Taylor, Susie King, site of, 76
Teachers' School of Science, 68
teaching as a profession, 15, 20, 26, 41, 47,
    56-57, 60, 67-68, 70, 76, 82. See also Boston
    Public School teachers.
telephone operators, 18; site of, 44-45; strike,
    44-45, 60
temperance movement, 14, 37
theater, 16, 21-22, 44, 57, 72, 90. See also actors,
    playwrights.
Termini, Maria, 49
Thurman, Sue Bailey, 36
Tianamin Memorial, 46
Ticknor & Fields Publishers, 19
Tontine Crescent/Franklin Place, site of, 22-23
Tozzer, Margaret Tenny, 54
trade unions, 13, 18, 44-45, 48, 50, 65, 75, 90
Transcendentalism, 35, 43-44
Tremont Temple, site of, 14-15
Trinity Church, 66
Truth, Sojourner, 76
Tsen, Wen-Ti, 46, 49
Tubman, Harriet, 37, 71, 77, 81; statue of
    (Step on Board), 77
Tucker, Sophie, site of, 26
Tuskegee Institute, 79, 80

Underground Railroad, 39, 77, 81, 83
unions. See trade unions.
Union United Methodist church, site of, 76
UNITE, 45
United South End Settlements, 77, 81, 85
Unity Towers Gardens, 89
Universalist churches, 28, 83
University of Massachusetts at Boston, 76
urban renewal, 70, 86

Vassar College, 69
Vazquez, Myrna, site of, 89
Vergoose, Elizabeth Foster, site of, 13
Victorian Society, 59
Villa Victoria Cultural Center, 88-89
Vilna Shul, site of, 37-38
Vincent, Mary, Vincent Memorial Hospital, 38
volunteerism, 70

Warren, Mercy Otis, site of, 17
Washington, George, 23
Waterston, Anna Cabot Lowell Quincy, 82
Weems, Katharine Lane, 58
Wellesley College, 25, 41, 48, 61
Wells, Kate Gannett, 26
Wheatley, Phillis, 64; sites of, 20, 45-46;
    statue of, 73
Whitman, Sarah Wyman, 71, 72, site of, 66
Whitney, Anne, 18, 29, 40, 63-64, 72;
    site of, 40
wildlife conservation, 58
Williams, Beatrice, 89
Williams, E. Virginia, 90
Wilson, Mary Evans, 81
Wimberly, Virginia, 90
Winsor School (Mary Pickard Winsor),
    site of, 60
Winthrop, Governor John, 19, 29
Winslow, Mary Chilton, 19
Woman's Era, 40

Woman's Journal, 14, 34, site of, 12. *See also*
    Massachusetts Woman Suffrage Association.
woman suffrage, 12, 14, 18, 30, 34, 48, 61, 65;
    anti-suffrage, 65.
Women's Army Corps, (WWII), 79
women's club movement, 12, 34, 40-41, 51
Women's Christian Temperance Movement, 14
women's education. *See* education.
Women's Education Association, 67-68
Women's Educational and Industrial Union,
    site of, 51
Women's International League for Peace and
    Freedom, site of, 61
Women's Lunch Place, site of, 69
Women's Relief Corps (Civil War), 76
Women's Republican Club, 81
Women's Service Club of Boston, site of, 81-82
Women's Trade Union League, 45, 48, 51, 65;
    sites of: 18, 50
Woods, Robert A., 85
World War I, 10, 11, 48, 61
World War II, 17-18, 45-46, 58, 61, 79, 89
writers, 11, 13-14, 17, 19, 20-23, 35-36, 37,
    39, 40-41, 40-46, 50-51, 63-65, 78, 79, 82.
    See also poets, playwrights.

Young Ladies Academy, 21
Young Women's Christian Association (YWCA),
    81; sites of, 49-50, 66-67

Zakrzewska, Dr. Marie, 38, 84

Nine Notable Women of Boston mural by Ellen Lanyon,
at the Boston Public Library (see page 64)

**Boston Women's Heritage Trail
Publications**

Dorchester Women's Heritage Trail. 2006.

*South End Walk: Cultural Diversity,
Activism, and Performing Arts.* 2005.

*The Ladies Walk: A Herstory Trail in Honor
of the Boston Women's Memorial.* 2005.

Women Artists in the Back Bay
(in conjunction with the Museum
of Fine Arts, Boston). 2004.

*Writing for Change: The Power of Women's
Words.* The Boston Women's Memorial
Curriculum by Sara Masucci, 2004.

"We Will Walk in Her Steps," West Roxbury
Women's Heritage Trail. 2001.

"Stepping Back," Roxbury Women's History
Trail. 1999.

*"Walk Her Way," A Boston Women's
Heritage Trail in the Neighborhood of
Charlestown, Massachusetts.* 1997.

*Voyages of Women: A Walk through the
Neighborhood of Lower Roxbury in Boston.*
1995.

*Biographies of Twenty Notable Boston
Women: A Curriculum Resource.*
Mary Smoyer, ed. 1993.

*Let Me Tell You Her Story: A Walk Through
History with the Women of Jamaica Plain.*
1992.

**Boston Women's Heritage Trail
22 Holbrook Street
Boston, MA 02130
617-522-2872**

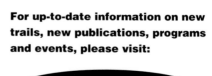

**For up-to-date information on new
trails, new publications, programs
and events, please visit:**

www.bwht.org